Scare
Your
Soul

Scare
Your
Soul

7 Powerful Principles to Harness Fear
and Lead Your Most Courageous Life

Scott Simon

balance

BOSTON   NEW YORK

A version of the story in "Maria Fills the Bag, Bean by Bean" on page 144 will appear in *Taking a Shot at Happiness* by Maria Baltazzi to be published by Post Hill Press.

Balance
Hachette Book Group
1290 Avenue of the Americas
New York, NY 10104
www.gcp-balance.com
https://twitter.com/gcpbalance

First Edition: December 2022

Balance is an imprint of Grand Central Publishing. The Balance name and logo are trademarks of Hachette Book Group, Inc.

The publisher is not responsible for websites (or their content) that are not owned by the publisher.

The Hachette Speakers Bureau provides a wide range of authors for speaking events. To find out more, go to www.hachettespeakersbureau.com or call (866) 376-6591.

Library of Congress Cataloging-in-Publication Data
Names: Simon, Scott, author.
Title: Scare your soul : 7 powerful principles to harness fear and lead your most courageous life / Scott Simon.
Description: First edition. | New York, NY : Balance, Hachette Book Group, 2022. | Includes index. |
Identifiers: LCCN 2022031729 | ISBN 9781538722916 (hardcover) | ISBN 9781538722930 (ebook)
Subjects: LCSH: Fear. | Courage. | Self-actualization (Psychology)
Classification: LCC BF575.F2 S486 2022 | DDC 152.4/6—dc23/eng/20220812
LC record available at https://lccn.loc.gov/2022031729

ISBNs: 978-1-5387-2291-6 (hardcover); 978-1-5387-2293-0 (ebook)

Printed in Canada

MRQ-T

10 9 8 7 6 5 4 3 2 1

To my parents, Bart and Sherry.
And to my children, Noah and T,
who have always been—and will always be—everything.

Acknowledgments

At 6:00 p.m. on a freezing December 21st evening in 2020, I was all alone, perched on a folding chair in the middle of Cleveland Yoga's darkened studio.

We were almost a year into the Covid-19 pandemic, and in an attempt to provide an extra dose of bravery during that confusing and fearful time, I was leading free courage meditations each week on Zoom. I sat calmly in the long rectangle of a studio, a brightly lit computer screen in front of me. I took a long, deep breath.

Just then, my phone began buzzing insistently.

Due to an email glitch, most of the regular meditation participants hadn't received the Zoom link, and they were all texting me to get it. So, while trying in vain to steady my own mind, I started to text them all back.

That's when a single email popped up onto my screen. It read:

Hi, Scott and team Scare Your Soul,

I'm the VP and Publisher of a new imprint at Hachette Book Group.

I've become familiar with Scare Your Soul and believe what you are doing is so necessary, especially during this turbulent time. I'd love to have a conversation with you about producing a book built around Scare Your Soul's work.

I thought to myself: "This has to be spam. What publisher actually reaches out to someone and asks them to write a book?"

So, I deleted it.

It wasn't until three days later that I somehow remembered that unexpected but intriguing email, redeeming it from my trash folder. That single email launched me on the journey of a lifetime, one that concluded with the publication of this book.

There is a well-known tradition of authors squirreling themselves away in their lonely writer's garret. And yes, while I did have many of those solitary writing days (often spent in abject terror as I contended with looming deadlines and soul-piercing crises of confidence), they were balanced beautifully by the collaboration with and inspiration from so many others.

And so, it is with greatest admiration that I thank my editor, Nana K. Twumasi, for believing in me. You provided the wise, steady guidance that brought the power of Scare Your Soul to life on the page. Thanks also go to the entire Balance, Hachette Book Group, and Grand Central Publishing teams, who are quite literally the best in the business.

Thank you to my literary agent, Lisa Leshne, and her entire team at the Leshne Agency for expert representation.

Thank you to the inspiring Scare Your Soul community: the team (I love you all); our passionate ambassadors who live our mission every day; and our tribe of "soulsters," who act on our challenges and inspire us with their successes. And thanks to my dear Sara Kelly, the very first person who believed in our movement enough to get her own Scare Your Soul tattoo.

To a wise and devastatingly talented writer: thank you, Christa Parravani. Thank you to Tiffany Hawk, Laurie Kincer, and Joelle Reizes for your expert guidance. And thank you to the Cuyahoga County Library System and its William N. Skirball Writers' Center, which became a second home to me.

Thank you to the brave souls who contributed their own personal stories to the book (or allowed me to interview them or tell their story): Kristina Ambrosia, Maria Baltazzi, Liz Bell, Wendy Diamond, Dahlia

Fisher, Claire Fullerton, Ron Gottfried, Jesse Harless, Carly Israel, Brett Kaufman, Jenn Lim, Abby Maslin, Simone Noble, Johanna Ratner, Dave Romanelli, Swan Sit, Lisa Skye, SaraMarie Thellman, Danielle Valenti, Ethan Zohn…and Jen Zivko of blessed memory.

Thank you to David and Caroline Selman for providing so much support, including a writer's haven in Sun Valley.

To many forever-friends who provided me special support and inspiration during these months of writing: Greg Abrams, Shana Auerbach, Seth Briskin, Christopher Celeste, Robert Crane, Norm Friedman, Sandra Graubard, Kristin Humbarger, Kate Kaura, Lauren Leader, Derek Martin, Lisa Mayers, Katie O'Keefe, Samara Smith, Ariana Starkman, Erica Starrfield, Kerri Tabasky, Sindy Warren, Whitney Wilkerson, Boriana Zaneva, and Noemi Zozaya.

To the positive psychology and mindfulness mentors who've taught me so much: Sharon Salzberg, Tal Ben-Shahar, and Maria Sirois.

To Samantha Baskind for your daily advice, support, and love.

To the best co-parent one could ever ask for: Laura Simon, I can't thank you enough for what you add to my life.

To Dana DeSantis, who handed me a card in the summer of 2021 that read "A Winner Is A Dreamer Who Never Gives Up," and who has inspired me every single day since.

To my family who support me unconditionally: Mom, Dad, Drew, Lily, Cole, Lo, Greg, Maya, Eli, Aunt Sue, Aunt Gail, Susan, Rich, Maryn, and the entire extended Carman clan.

And finally, like anyone reading this book, I carry within my insides a multitude: I am a son, a co-parent, a friend, a lover, a striver, an appreciator of vintage guitars and freezing cold martinis, a shy extrovert, a yogi, a world traveler, a wannabe boxer, a reader, an entrepreneur, a coach. But at my very core, I am but one thing. I am a *father*. My deepest experiences of life—and the courage that has called to me with every step along the way—have been as "Dad" to Noah and Teilah Simon.

To them I say thank you. I love you with all my heart.

Your Private Online Companion Journal

We have created an easy and free online location for you to privately record your answers to the book's prompts and exercises, keep track of your Scare Your Soul challenge successes, and reflect while reading each chapter.

To access the Companion Journal, scan the unique QR code:

1. Open the camera app on your phone.
2. Focus the camera on the QR code.
3. Follow the instructions to create your free profile and begin using your Journal.

Scare
Your
Soul

Contents

PART IV
Moving Forward: The Journey Ahead

Introduction

Scare Your Soul: \ sker yər sōl \

Noun:

1. A courage movement that empowers small acts of tackling fear.
2. A way of life that is brave, daring, spirited, lighthearted, and full of energy.
3. A tribe of fear-chasers.

On a small stretch of Coventry Road, between the head shops and the secondhand vinyl stores, a cold wind carried with it scraps of concert announcements and long-over happy-hour specials. Even with that crisp breeze blowing as I walked, sweat slid down my temples. The restaurant had just come into view.

More than a dozen people—the hardiest of the Sunday-brunch-aficionados—were already lined up in the wide open plaza by the restaurant's front door. Hands jammed in their pockets against the wind, they were likely fantasizing over the restaurant's famous Belgian waffles and tofu scrambles.

And me?

I was about to Scare My Soul.

The restaurant's romantic name—the *Inn on Coventry*—could easily conjure up images of a warmly lit London pub or a B&B tucked back beyond a covered bridge in Vermont, but on that May morning in 2016, the inn didn't feel in any way romantic; in fact, it felt more like a death trap.

And as I approached the plaza, gripping the handle of my guitar case, one lone question raced to mind:

Why in the hell do I do this to myself?

Yes, all of this terror—the angst and the sweat—were completely of my choosing.

You see, I've had some big-ticket adventures since I became a fear-chaser. I've taken on my fear of heights by skydiving from fourteen thousand feet, negotiated multimillion-dollar deals with tough and cynical real estate developers, navigated an unexpected maze of rioters and tear gas in an Athens city square to hop right on the first boat headed to Mykonos, officiated an impromptu wedding in the middle of a jam-packed restaurant, and sought out a famous healer living far up in the misty mountains of Bali.

But, over the years, I've discovered that those big, gaudy actions are not what make us.

It is the daily work.

It is the intentional choice we make to walk into the fire of fear with the hope of growing from its discomfort—not flinging ourselves out of planes or quitting our jobs and moving to Tuscany— that fosters a flourishing life.

Which is why, that morning on Coventry Road, I chose to tackle my thirty-five-year fear of singing in public by singing in front of a group of strangers.

. . .

I actually loved to sing when I was young. There was only one snag: I have a terrible voice. No false modesty here. *I can't sing to save my life.* No matter how hard I try, my voice bounces erratically from sharp to flat, never quite reaching its intended target.

But for most of my childhood, no one cared. So, I sang with gusto. To me, it felt like pure, unbridled joy.

And then, as sometimes happens, an authority figure changed me. Our fourth grade choir was in final preparations for our big concert, and our substitute choir teacher, decked out in a Hawaiian shirt despite the freezing Ohio temperatures, was working feverishly to get us ready for the concert's big finale. We would be blowing our parents' minds by singing a full-class rendition of *The Music Man's* "Seventy-Six Trombones."

But my voice seemed to be getting in the way. Our Magnum P.I. wannabe had given me one line to sing solo, and I just couldn't get the tune right. When my part was fast approaching, I would choke up. As I got more embarrassed, he got hotter around the collar.

On the third run-through, I could barely croak above a whisper. That's when he flipped his lid. I remember his old-school red Hawaiian shirt with its big green palm tree leaves coming right at me.

"You! You're literally wasting all of our time," he hissed in front of everyone. "You know what? Forget it. Why don't you go ahead and mouth the words? Let everyone else sing."

It may seem humorous now, but I could feel my face burning red in embarrassment. I stood like a statue, unable to move. And in those few moments, I created a new story: *I don't love singing, I hate it. I am terrible at it. It can only bring me pain and embarrassment.*

To my recollection, I don't think I ever sang in public again.

Until the day I finally decided to confront my demon and rewrite that story.

· · ·

I found an empty spot on the plaza by the restaurant's front door. The nay-saying voice in my head, a constant companion on my many courage escapades, started to chatter:

You are going to fail. Hard.

Why are you doing this?

You are going to embarrass yourself like never before, buddy.

This is the moment where I shut down the monologue. I swiped the sweat from my forehead and conjured up the image of my choir teacher and his palm frond shirt. I took a deep breath and strummed the first chord of "The Boxer."

Now, here is the God's honest truth: I was *awful*. Simon and Garfunkel would have every right to be outraged. From the first verse, there were awkward stares from the crowd. A vibe of annoyance.

But by the second song, I felt more comfortable and my enthusiasm started to win the crowd over. I spied a few smiles. A youngster ran forward with a crumpled dollar bill, tossing it in my open case. Laughter erupted. My sister, Lo, who has a uniquely stunning voice and was there to support me, joined in. Ten minutes later, I strummed my last chord, and with that my impromptu public concert was officially over.

As the final applause died down, that very sensation I crave overcame me: a rich broth of pride, exhilaration, and confidence coursing through my veins.

Musically, the experience was a travesty, but in reaching deep inside and finding the courage to confront my fear, it was a triumph. For thirty-five years, I didn't sing alone in public. Now, after just ten minutes, I wanted to do it all over again.

As soon as possible.

I had just scared my soul.

Scare Your Soul Gets Its Wings

> Genuinely happy people do not just sit around being content. They make things happen. —DAN BUETTNER

I was so pumped about my fear-tackling experience on Coventry that I wrote a single Facebook post about it.

I see myself as a "connector," someone who loves to link people with new ideas, with each other, and with ways to make their lives happier. I thought the post might inspire a few friends to do what I had just done in their own lives.

But that one post was shared—literally—around the world.

Strangers from Iran, China, Brazil, Kazakhstan, India, Poland, and Chile sent me congratulatory messages. *(All for singing badly in front of a restaurant!)* By the following weekend, people around the world were tackling their own scary acts and sharing them with me. They didn't parrot *my* challenge; they chose ones that were meaningful to *them*.

They tackled hard and scary things. They kicked off long-dormant dream projects, held tough conversations, booked adventurous trips, stopped drinking alcohol, signed up for an interesting course, asked for help from a friend. Many said "yes" to things that set their hearts on fire.

Scare Your Soul was starting to take flight.

．　．　．

Today, we have thousands of participants and dozens of volunteer ambassadors across the globe—representing a beautiful diversity of ages, genders, and backgrounds—all living the powerful commitment to engage in small acts of courage.

As Scare Your Soul's founder, I am blessed to be able to develop challenges for people to become braver. I support people around the world as they quit unfulfilling jobs, start their own companies, leave toxic relationships, get married, launch innovative social projects, hold space for tough conversations, bring their art into the world, begin healing from past traumas, reconnect with lost friends, and free themselves from the burden of anger and bitterness.

I've steeped myself in powerful methodologies that motivate bravery and harness fear, and I've studied the cutting-edge research and data developed in the new-but-powerful field of positive psychology.

I've learned what works.

And most importantly, I live a Scare Your Soul life myself.

I willingly dance with my fears every single day.

It's All About Courageous Action

> One can choose to go back toward safety or forward toward
> growth. Growth must be chosen, again and again…
>
> —ABRAHAM MASLOW

You and I confront both real and self-created fears constantly.

Many—especially after a pandemic—have responded by trying like hell to bolster their comfort zones in an effort to stay safe and sane. In a cruel twist of fate, however, our penchant for avoiding our fears actually makes us even more fearful. We forget our dreams. We stop pushing the envelope. We stop growing. *Just think about all of the love, joy, connection, growth, adventure, creation, and innovation that never sees the light of day…simply because we are afraid.*

Consider this: The tiny hatchling only learns to fly after its mother pushes it from its nest. The mother understands that it is only through that first terrifying drop toward the ground that the chick will learn that it, yes, can truly fly.

The poet Mary Oliver famously posed the question "What is it you plan to do with your one wild and precious life?"[1]

Here is the *Scare Your Soul* version: Are you finally ready to leap out of your nest to go find that one wild and precious life?

This Book, You, and Me

> A ship in harbor is safe, but that is not what ships are built for.
>
> —JOHN AUGUSTUS SHEDD

My sincere hope is that this book is a roadmap on your journey to an audacious life.

Throughout its pages, you'll experience a tapestry of stories, science and research, writing prompts, and thought exercises.

You'll hear from more than a dozen real people, in their own words, who chose one courageous act that changed their lives. You'll find ways to challenge yourself to grow. You'll dislodge old beliefs and fears you thought you had forgotten. And you'll dive deep into seven areas of life that will be brought to full bloom. At times, I share specific ways our brains process fear and how they can be rewired toward positivity and enhanced confidence.

And in the spirit of boldness, I'll ask you to join me in something unique:

From this point forward, let's ditch the antiquated, preconceived notion of you (as reader) and me (as author).

Let's do this together.

Here's my personal commitment: I will share my knowledge of fear and courage with you. I'll share, unvarnished, my past, my flaws, and my struggles, and I'll share my values and passions. You'll get all of me.

And this is all I ask of you:

- Bring an open mind and an adventurous spirit.
- Have a journal or pad of paper at hand.
- Use this book as a tool: Reflect on your dreams. Use the writing prompts. Do the Scare Your Soul challenges.
- Finally and most importantly—commit to raising your anchor and setting sail from your safe harbor.

If you are ready to engage in the deep work of knowing yourself, understanding your own fears, and taking sincere action, then you and I have come together at the right place and time.

Let's begin.

PART I

Getting Started

Working Your Courage Muscles

CHAPTER 1

The Eight Words That Changed My Life

Not everything that is faced can be changed. But nothing can be changed until it is faced. —JAMES BALDWIN

If you could choose any superpower, what would yours be? From the age of six onward, I knew without a doubt what I would pick.

My choice wasn't about possessing crazy superstrength, being able to see through walls with X-ray vision, or flying at supersonic speed high above the earth. What I really wanted—above all else— was to be *invisible*.

Despite the warmth I felt in the safe cocoon of my close family, my chronic shyness coupled with being physically and verbally bullied led to a pervasive fear that took over my life.

It wasn't until much later in life, in my early twenties, through what I can only describe as an epiphany (on an airplane, no less), that I finally woke up. It was at that moment that I truly started living my life.

We all possess a story about what brought us to important moments in our lives. You have yours, and I have mine. And, although this book is *all about you*, I hope you will trust me, know me, and join me on this journey. To that end, here is my story.

Mine is one of a childhood spent running from fear, and an adulthood spent chasing it.

Black-and-White Polaroids

If there were ever an encyclopedia entry entitled "young couple in love," next to it there would be a slightly grainy, black-and-white, 1964 Polaroid of my parents, Bart and Sherry.

They met in an aisle of the Michigan State University bookstore the first week of my mom's freshman year. My dad and his friend chatted up my mom and her friend, netting a double date for that night. In a strange twist of fate, my dad was matched with my mom's friend at the beginning of the evening, but within a couple hours, my parents righted the course of the universe (and ensured my birth) by ditching their dates for one another.

Years later, I found an old album of photos from those early days that revealed my mom as a buoyant coed with a stylish bob haircut. She looked beautiful, almost regal, pressed against my father, a slim, handsome young man in glasses gazing at her, seemingly delighted just to be by her side.

Soon after graduation, they married, stitching together two families from different worlds: my mom's family was Protestant and from the small working-class town of Marion, Ohio, and my dad's family was Jewish, from the socially conscious Cleveland suburb of Shaker Heights.

They began their married lives in Detroit. Working as high school teachers meant that finances were tight, and they saved as much as they could, stashing away a few dollars each month in an envelope labeled "date night." On these highly anticipated evenings, they would talk about their future—about the self-confident kids they wanted to have one day—while ordering all they could afford: two glasses of ice water and one hamburger, cut evenly down the middle.

Two years later, on the balmy summer solstice morning in 1969, I was born.

From the very beginning, we had an abundance of love in our home. In that stable environment, I spent my early years as a bright and loving, albeit shy, child. My teachers remember me best as that kid who would be the first to comfort another boy who was sad, or who sat down next to the girl who was new to the class.

Life in those early days, often spent with my brother, Drew, and sister, Lo, was idyllic. And, other than my parents and siblings, and my friend David (whom I met in the sandbox outside our apartment complex when we were two), my closest confidants in those early years were my grandparents.

They had, I can say with utter conviction, the greatest impact on who I was then and who I am today. They were polar opposites of one another, but each contributed something monumental.

On my mother's side, there was my silver-haired, Irish, piano-playing grandmother, Peg, who grew up in the one-street town of Holton, Michigan, and taught me a passion for music and a love of making people happier. My bighearted grandfather Ted (we called him "Peachy") was a Whirlpool executive who boasted the heartiest belly laugh and gave me bear hugs that I was convinced would split me in two. It was from Peachy that I learned a commitment to expressing love without hesitation or reservation.

On my father's side, I was taught the value of manners and hard work by my elegantly sophisticated grandfather, Sanford, who had stumbled as a would-be inventor but emerged as an esteemed architect and engineer. And I learned the virtue of courage in the face of adversity from my vivacious grandmother who, at the age of nine, escaped Poland on the verge of war, stepped off the steamer *Mauretania* onto Ellis Island, changed her name from Golda to Grace, and never looked back.

I am fortunate to have grown up amidst some of the greatest people I will ever know.

And they loved *me* with abandon.

Thrown Out of the Nest

What seemed like my lovable attributes at home—being quiet, sensitive, and loving— didn't translate when I left the warm confines for school.

As early as I can remember, I felt the sting of not being able to connect or make good friends. I was the shortest boy in my grade. I was always picked last for any team or physical activity. And I was shy.

Life got worse when two boys at my school saw my quietness as a sign of weakness. They would taunt me, yelling "shrimp" and "loser." They would swing me around in circles and send me spiraling off into the bushes. Once, one of them attacked me with a long metal reflector pole, which somehow found its way into my mouth. I spat out blood for the rest of the day.

At home, I hid the bruises—visible and invisible —from my parents and grandparents. Instead, I turned inward.

In middle school, when asked to speak in class, my throat would close up and I would barely stutter out the answer. By the time I entered Orange High School, fear and anxiety had taken an even stronger hold. Lunchtimes were the worst. I would join the cafeteria line, adding a hamburger, a side of orange-tinted curly fries, and a small carton of chocolate milk to my tray. Then, nervously navigating my way through the tables full of chattering kids, I would seek out just one welcoming glance that would save me from eating my lunch all alone yet again.

Most every day, I ended up doing just that. I felt lonely, embarrassed, and unworthy.

We all have our ways of coping with our own challenging emotions, and in the fear trifecta of fight, flight, or freeze, mine was "flight" every single day.

In eleventh grade, I transferred from my public high school purgatory to Gilmour Academy, a small Catholic school near home. I would choose the same "flight strategy" in college: In my sophomore year, I would eventually transfer from the socially adventurous Tulane University in New Orleans to Skidmore College in upstate New York. I remained hopeful that some new location would somehow change my life.

Change *me*.

But change couldn't come from a new city or school; as I would learn soon enough, real change is an inside job.

. . .

It took me five years to finish college, and as I walked across the Saratoga Performing Arts Center stage with a Skidmore degree in English literature, I felt the familiar pang of unworthiness yet again. Unlike most of my fellow graduates, I had no job waiting in the wings. No plan for what would come next.

In a desperate move on my behalf, my father called in a favor with an old friend: Joel was a professional at a local fundraising organization and had an idea for me. "Actually, it is an extraordinary opportunity," Joel told my dad, "but only if Scott is willing to take a risk."

That risk was a job teaching English to elderly Holocaust survivors in Israel.

For six months, I would have to live in a tiny room in an apartment with an Israeli family. There would most likely be very little English spoken around me, and I would work long hours with no pay. The balance of the year would be spent on two kibbutzim, communal collectives, where I would also work long hours for no pay.

But, Joel said, "This could all be the most meaningful work he will ever do."

So I agreed. In my mind, I had no choice. This was my only shot.

The Epiphany

Several weeks later, I slung a backpack over my shoulder, hugged my parents goodbye, and boarded a flight from Cleveland to Kennedy Airport.

Awaiting the flight to Tel Aviv, I walked the long concourse in a daze. What the hell was I doing? At an airport bookstore, I bought a spiral notebook in an attempt to capture my oversized emotions on paper. I shoved the notebook into my bag as I made my way down the tarmac and onto the largest plane I'd ever seen.

On the plane, my heart rushing, I tried to push past a mass of humanity, navigating my oversized backpack through a phalanx of bearded Orthodox Jews, groups of teens in matching T-shirts, and people yelling or laughing (or both?) in languages I couldn't understand.

I found my seat. I was in a panic.

Those all-too-familiar feelings of being scared, invisible, and "not enough" knotted in my stomach. The voice in my head was impossible to ignore.

Why am I doing this?

I am a failure! I will always be a failure.

I can't handle this!

A flight attendant reminded us to fasten our seat belts. The lights dimmed. Any last opportunity to turn back was gone. The plane lifted off, and my heart raced. Up to that moment, remaining invisible in my own life had meant trying to stay safe. None of it had worked.

I had only kept myself from living! Something had to change! I could not live the rest of my life like this!

In a completely unconscious moment, I pulled the notebook from my backpack. I flipped it open on the tray table in front of me. Uncapping my pen, my heart in my throat, I wrote one single phrase, a famous quote by Eleanor Roosevelt that I had once read during my studies at Skidmore. To this day, I don't know how it emerged from the depths of my soul. But in the height of my fear and panic, its eight words tumbled from my pen:

Do one thing every day that scares you.

I sat for a long time, looking hard at those words.

Inside me, something shifted.

Do one thing every day that scares you.

I knew what it meant for me. It was a directive. A mandate.

On that EL AL jet, flying high above the life I had led for twenty-one years, I made a commitment to myself. For the upcoming year, I would choose to tackle one thing every day that scared me. I knew full well that scaring myself would mean intentionally seeking out my edges, searching for my discomfort. And standing firm in that discomfort.

This was my chance to change. This was my chance to wake up and finally start living my life.

$$\cdot \quad \cdot \quad \cdot$$

Ten hours later, I tumbled off the plane into Ben Gurion Airport.

We were funneled into a large hall to retrieve our bags. Although it was past 1:00 a.m., the room was uncomfortably hot; strains of Hebrew and Arabic reverberated. I felt someone's carry-on bag knock into my backpack.

I turned and saw an older gentleman with an elegant air despite his rumpled khakis and button-down shirt. Like the rest of us, he was trying to enter the scrum at the baggage carousel. I looked back again, and our eyes met.

Before that day, I would have immediately looked away, fearing an interaction. Instead, I took a deep breath and smiled. I said hello and asked if I could help get his bag for him.

He smiled back. "That would be kind. Thank you."

As we waited for the carousel to begin spitting out suitcases, we talked. I told him it was my first time in the country (about which he was overjoyed), and he told me he was a retired architect, arriving back in Tel Aviv after visiting a sick friend in New York. His name was Yitzchak.

He looked up at the baggage carousel and pointed out a black suitcase with a pocket square knotted around its handle. As I hauled it off the conveyer belt and placed it in front of him, Yitzchak was busy writing on the back of his plane ticket. He handed it to me.

"Here," he said. "This is my number. You must come to Tel Aviv sometime and have dinner with my wife and me."

It was my first new friendship in years.

Searching for Meaning

I was picked up from the airport by a loquacious Canadian ex-pat, Morty (a friend of Joel's and a brilliant future mentor of mine), and driven to the lower-income neighborhood that would become my new home. In the near darkness, Neve Sharett was barren and brown. Morty and I trudged up four flights of stairs to the small apartment of the Israeli family: Tzipi, Amnon, and their daughter, Serai. My new family, despite our language barrier, was loving and kind to me from that very first minute.

The following morning, I walked those dusty brown streets flanked by apartment buildings studded with clotheslines all the way to the Saltzman-Wuliger senior center, where I would be teaching my classes. It was also the day that I began my courage commitment.

Everything in this new life felt overwhelming, so it wasn't hard to fulfill my objective. I started with the simplest of actions:

- Learning my first five words in Hebrew (*ken, lo, shalom, todah, slicha—yes, no, hello/goodbye, thank you,* and *excuse me*) and using them at home with my very proud new family
- Memorizing the unfamiliar, and at times intimidating, streets of Neve Sharett
- Taking a city bus alone for the first time
- Leading my first class in front of twenty elderly Holocaust survivors

In most cases, I totally failed in my first attempts.

I was dreadfully slow at learning Hebrew, which, in writing, continued to look like hieroglyphics on acid to me. I got lost daily in the meandering streets. My first time on an Israeli public bus was comical, as I was pushed aside by a headstrong Israeli grandmother (I would soon learn that pushing and shoving to get on a Tel Aviv bus is nothing short of a national rite of passage).

But my experience with my elderly students was transformative. I was in awe of the joy they radiated despite having endured the atrocities of the Holocaust. They showered me with so much love, and teaching them sustained me through those bumpy first weeks of this new, scary life.

One late afternoon after class, in the senior center's tiny second-floor library, I found a dog-eared copy of a book in English. It was Viktor Frankl's *Man's Search for Meaning*. In the sunlit afternoons after class ended, I would sit on a bench under a grove of trees outside the doors of the senior center.

I couldn't put the book down. Frankl's story captivated me.

In the early 1940s, he was a respected Viennese Jewish doctor and psychologist. In 1942, just nine months after marrying the love of his life, Tilly Grosser, he and his entire family were rounded up and sent to the Theresienstadt concentration camp. It was there that Frankl came face-to-face with unspeakable horror. It was also where he lost the first of many family members, his father dying of starvation and pneumonia. In 1944, Frankl was transported to Auschwitz, where his mother and brother died in the camp's gas chambers. His beloved Tilly died of typhus in the Bergen-Belsen camp.

Despite the horror, the degradation, and the death, Frankl wrote about his own epiphany in which he somehow was able to find—within his own consciousness—a space of courageous peace. His words etched themselves like finely stained glass into my brain as I sat on the bench, Holocaust survivors walking by me just feet away:

Everything can be taken from a man but one thing: the last of the human freedoms—to choose one's attitude in any given set of circumstances, to choose one's own way....When we are no longer able to change a situation, we are challenged to change ourselves.[1]

This power over adversity, over death, over the unknown, over fear—*it was all about making choices.*

If Frankl could take control of his life by changing his mindset within the worst circumstances imaginable, I knew deep in my bones that I could, too.

I was on the right path!

This mission to tackle my fears was about to intensify.

The Power of Courageous Action

I bid a fond farewell to my beloved host family, now on my way to work as a volunteer on two *kibbutzim* (one in the Jezreel Valley in the country's lush hills in the north and another just on the outskirts of Jerusalem). When I wasn't working, I traveled the country alone, buoyed by a solid core of confidence and burgeoning self-love. And I kept my eye on my prize: one thing every day that scared me.

When I tackled something new and scary, I recorded it in my spiral notebook:

- I climbed Mount Sinai at midnight, scared out of my wits when I got completely lost on my way up, and was thankfully directed to the top by a kind shepherd tending his flock in the moonlight.
- I tackled my fear of deep water by diving into the ink-colored waves of the famous "Blue Hole" in the Gulf of Aqaba (nicknamed the world's most dangerous diving site).
- I opened my eyes and mind to the sites held sacred by religions not my own: exploring solo the majesty of the Baha'i Gardens and the winding, narrow stone path of the Via Dolorosa,

inhaling the incense of the Church of the Holy Sepulcher, stepping into the Sea of Galilee.

- I spent evenings with residents of the Arab village—Ein Rafa—that lay next to my Jerusalem kibbutz, drinking glasses of sweet cardamom tea, and listening, enraptured, to their family histories, so different from mine.
- As someone who had once been unable to participate in my own grade school classes, I committed to listening, learning, and speaking my own truth. I conversed with nomadic Muslim Bedouin farmers in their open-sided tents, learned football chants while dancing on bar tables with English backpackers, prayed alongside fellow Jews from around the world, our hands pressed against the note-filled crags of the Western Wall.
- I pushed through the trauma of a failed high school romance and fell hard for Masha, a bubbly new immigrant from Kyiv; she fell hard for me right back, with tiny snippets of Hebrew and late-night kisses in an abandoned kibbutz bomb shelter as our only forms of communication.

On my last night in Israel, I sat alone in the ruins of an old Crusader castle on a hill above the kibbutz and overlooking Jerusalem.

In the translucent light that seemed so exclusive to that ancient city, I peered out over the horizon and smiled.

This year had given me something of infinite value.

Through small ways each and every day, I had made the choices Viktor Frankl wrote about so powerfully.

I had taken my life back. I would return to the States impassioned.

Instead of running from my fears, I would now be chasing them.

The Road Ahead

Years later, I found myself with a lavalier mic pinned to the lapel of my dark-blue sport coat, walking the length of a stage. I was about to give a TEDx Talk with good friend and happiness incubator co-founder, Jen Margolis.

I looked out over row after row of faces. High-def cameras were recording every single word and gesture.

I peered into the bright spotlight and thought of those bullies, of me spinning off like a top into the bushes, those lonely elementary school hallways and cafeterias, the bathrooms that doubled as my hiding places. I thought of that scared-shitless kid who couldn't speak in class without stammering. The kid who ran to stay safe.

The one who only wanted to be invisible.

That same kid—now forty-three years old—was about to shed another layer of invisibility. Standing in front of a sold-out audience, about to give a talk about leading a thriving life full of meaning and purpose.

Since the moment I opened the journal on the EL AL jet, I've done things unimaginable to me in the life I had prior. And I credit it all to my commitment to harnessing my fears and taking the risks.

Pushing comfort zones has become my muse, and living my life like an adventure has become my guidebook.

To be clear, I'm not an expert on courage or fear. What I do possess, however, as the founder of Scare Your Soul, are years of helping people to be just a little more courageous in their lives.

And what I've learned over these years is magic in a bottle: When we take small steps of acting courageously in our lives, we flourish. We actually begin to live what Elizabeth Gilbert calls "an ignited life."[2]

I want you to have the best, most ignited, most hair-on-fire, most passionate life. Because when we each individually lead that life, more great ideas happen…more truth and social justice arise…more businesses are created…more healthy relationships are fostered… more children see role models full of integrity and bravery.

You *can* change.

You can overcome feeling fearful, stuck, unsure, and lost.

You can lead a joyful, adventurous, meaningful, and connected life.

And it begins with you making the same decision that I did that fateful day on a plane: to choose courage consistently and with zest.

And to *do one thing every day that scares you.*

CHAPTER 2

The Power of the Blank Page

The best time to plant a tree was 20 years ago. The second best time is now. —CHINESE PROVERB

Think about how it might feel to open up a brand-new journal.

After cracking the spine just a little to write your name inside the cover, you discover a single, clean, blank page. There are no previous entries. No doodles in the margins. And you can't flip forward to see what's ahead.

It's just you, your pen, and a fresh start.

And there can be a lot of genuinely valid fears represented by a fresh start:

What if I don't know what comes next?

What if I do something wrong?

What if change brings something I don't want?

I would argue that the greatest things that have ever happened in our world history—and in our own lives—have existed in that space of the scary unknown. When our well-laid plans go awry. When we have to act on instinct, on our core values. When everything feels limitless because, well…in that moment, everything is indeed limitless.

I am here to tell you that—*in this very moment*—there is a blank page open in front of you.

Take stock in how you feel right now. You may, in some way, feel limited.

You have a blank page.

You may feel constrained by your age, job, bank account, or responsibilities, unjustly defined by your background, how you were raised and by whom, your past traumas, or your deep regrets.

You may feel stuck, frightened, alone, or unheard.

You have a blank page.

And even if you have no damn clue what it is you want to write in the next chapter of your life, but you know somewhere deep inside that you need a change—you too have a blank page.

This book is your blank page.

How Are You, *Really*?

> Listening is about being present, not just about being quiet.
>
> —KRISTA TIPPETT

As Harvard professor Dr. Tal Ben-Shahar looked out at us, he must have seen one hell of a motley crew: 120 students, fanned out across a large rectangular hall, seated on the floor with laptops and journals perched precariously on our laps and knees. A touch of a Hebrew accent was evident in his voice as it echoed in greeting off the red brick walls and tall, timber-lined ceiling.

It was the very first day of a positive-psychology certificate program that would change many of our lives. Mine included.

Now, learning about "the science of happiness" may seem like a mild-enough pursuit, and, at five foot seven, with a slight build and humble affect, Tal didn't present the most imposing stature. But I can assure you the concepts he taught us were Herculean.

Tal taught us tangible tools to help people lead happier lives, to be more courageous, to bounce back from loss more quickly. He shared cutting-edge research and intriguing concepts from psychologists and theologians. But one of the most powerful lessons he taught us came on that very first day.

If we wanted to really create massive shifts in our lives, we first needed to know ourselves deeply and then vulnerably and bravely share our truth with others. That is where real, honest, powerful change starts. Our example that day was a very simple exercise.

It was called "How are you, *really*?"

Tal asked us to pair with another student (cue the awkward effort to find a partner) and sit together face-to-face. The instructions were brief: One of us was to ask our partner, "How are you, *really*?" The respondent would be required to answer that question. The kicker: One had to answer it for three full minutes without stopping. Then we'd switch.

Invariably, the first comments arose in cocktail-chatter style.

"Well, I'm doing fine. I'm loving this."

"I'm kinda tired today. I was up late talking with my roommate."

"I'm gonna go for a run later… can't wait…"

But as the seconds and minutes passed, and the small talk became exhausted, we had no choice but to say what was *really* going on with us. The deeper realities of our lives appeared from the mist of superficiality, and the talk got real.

"I'm feeling intimidated in this program. I'm thinking of dropping out."

"My dad is sick at home. I'm really worried about him, and I don't know how to help."

"I am so glad that you were paired with me. I find you so interesting and really wanted to get to know you better."

It was in those vulnerable moments that magic happened. That's where friendships were born; that's where iron-clad allegiances began; that's where support became steadfast.

Makes sense, right?

When we literally couldn't modulate our ability to stay safe and superficial, we had to dive deep. And deep is where ALL of life's good stuff resides.

So, to begin your process of diving deep in your own life—and in true partnership between you and me—take a full three minutes to write from your soul.

I ask you, How are you... *really*?

_____

_____

_____

_____

_____

_____

_____

_____

_____

_____

_____

_____

_____

_____

_____

_____

_____

_____

_____

CHAPTER 3

Waking Up to the Dreams We've Forgotten

You may say I'm a dreamer, but I'm not the only one.

—JOHN LENNON

For a shy, quiet ten-year-old like me, Joan Silberbach's basement was a wonderland.

Joan was a hippieish former high school art teacher who taught after-school supplemental painting, design, and papier-mâché to kids who either wanted to hone their artistic abilities...or whose parents wanted a place to keep their kids occupied before their busy workday ended.

Once a week, I'd take a different school bus to her house, pull out the chocolate chip cookie my mom had stashed in the bottom of my school bag that morning, and descend Joan's basement steps into another world.

The long, subterranean room was packed with a variety of stretched, starched-white canvases, vises and grips, tools of all vintages, buckets of glue, and tubes of paint rolled up tight like drained toothpaste. I'd raise my nose and give a sniff. The air was heady with the unforgettable trinity of linseed oil, white gesso, and soldering iron smoke.

The first year I spent in that safe and magical space, I created dozens of projects. But by far my most coveted piece was a life-size replica of John Lennon's black-and-white 1963 Rickenbacker 325 electric guitar made completely of papier-mâché.

John Lennon was my hero. For someone like me—the kid who turned beet red even thinking about speaking in front of a group— John's performance at Shea Stadium in front of tens of thousands of screaming fans bestowed upon him pure deity status in my young eyes. I would watch the concert on our boxy old home VCR, and the image of him smiling and strumming amidst sheer pandemonium was burned into my brain. Being a rock star, to me, had to be the ultimate fantasy.

Joan Silberbach had taught me the basics of papier-mâché: first, create the skeleton out of chicken wire; then dredge thin strips of newspaper through glue; then lay them across in a well-defined pattern. After weeks of diligence, I applied the final coat of black and white paint. The Lennon Rickenbacker was ready.

After bringing it home and unveiling it to my family, I carried it upstairs. I locked my door. Only I knew why I had put so much effort into this project.

I grabbed the belt from my maroon robe as a guitar strap and slung the Rickenbacker 325 over my shoulder. I centered myself in front of the wide mirror on my wall and carefully placed the needle on the spinning record on the desk below.

After a few crackles, the first sounds from the Beatles' *White Album* emerged. The landing of an airplane, its wheels screeching on impact, followed by the up-tempo piano and guitar of "Back in the U.S.S.R."

Ooooooo…Flew in from Miami Beach BOAC. Didn't get to bed last night.

I leapt around my room. Strumming, lip-synching. In that moment I wasn't the shy, unwanted kid. I was a rock god! I felt powerful, talented, wanted.

That was my dream.

I'm proud to say that the dream of being a rock star continues on to this day. Let me explain.

The Power of Dreams

> All human beings are also dream beings. Dreaming ties all mankind together. —JACK KEROUAC

Our dreams are our truest desires decked out in blinking Las Vegas neon.

Sometimes existing in our conscious mind and sometimes arising in those hazy, half-lit moments of fantasy, they reveal what we really want and value. They are an internal compass, guiding us to what really excites and fuels us. Sometimes our dreams are valiant and pure; sometimes they are private and prurient.

But they are who we are at our core. If we choose to pay attention to them, of course.

> **Note:** *When I refer to dreams, I am not talking about the recurring one you have at midnight about a mannequin chasing you naked down the produce aisles at your local grocery store. The dreams we'll work with in this book are the daydreams, fantasies, or wish states that occupy our minds at times when we feel limitless. Just imagine me on stage playing guitar with Pearl Jam; you get the idea.*

Scare Your Soul Challenge: Unpacking One of Your Dreams

This is your first Scare Your Soul Challenge!

Here we go: Think of a daydream or fantasy you've experienced consistently over your life. If you don't have one, just choose a more recent one that feels powerful to you. Note: The more awkward, the wilder, the scarier it feels to write out, the better. That means you are really digging deep. Briefly write out the dream, when you might experience it, and how it makes you feel.

As an example, here's mine.

One consistent (or powerful) dream:

I'm standing off to the side of the stage at the Hollywood Bowl. It's totally packed—full capacity. There's electricity in the air and the crowd goes bonkers as Pearl Jam takes the stage. Mike McCready, Pearl Jam's lead guitarist, is really tired from this long tour and needs a night off. Eddie Vedder looks my way at the side of the stage and gives me a wink. He motions to Mike's unused electric guitar. I walk on stage, strap on the guitar, and we launch into the greatest high-decibel version of "Even Flow" ever.

Five words that describe how the dream makes me feel:

connected, alive, loved, creative, immortal

Your turn.

One consistent (or powerful) dream:

_____

_____

_____

_____

And five words that describe how the dream makes you feel:

_____

_____

Taking One Step

> The future belongs to those who believe in the beauty of
> their dreams. —ELEANOR ROOSEVELT

Every few months, our ambassador team hits the road and brings a courage challenge out into a community.

One of my favorites is called the "Dream Table."

It's simple. Our volunteers partner with a local coffeehouse and set up a folding table out front early on a Sunday morning. We tape a few balloons to the table to rock a festive vibe, pull up a couple of chairs, and start smiling at everyone walking by.

Inevitably, we don't get much attention at first. People glance over and quickly look away as if we are trying to sell them life insurance. But after a while, one or two curious people will approach. We ask these brave souls, "Name one dream that you've had for years but haven't done anything about."

You can see the change on their faces immediately.

They go to a completely different place. They look upward, musing, smiling to themselves as they reinhabit old fantasies.

I dream of starting the next Google.

I dream of quitting it all and being a painter.

I dream of paragliding over the Grand Canyon at sunset.

I dream of being an orthopedic surgeon like my mom.

I dream of traveling through Europe solo for a month.

I dream of playing with elephants and swimming with sharks.

It's light. It's fun. And then we have a follow-up question:

What is one small action you can take in the next twenty-four hours that would move you closer to that dream?

That's where roadblocks appear.

I could never afford to do that.

I'm not smart enough to be a surgeon.

I can't leave my job.

My spouse would never agree to that.

It's just a fantasy, not reality.

One young woman said to me, "I want to be a philanthropist. But it will never happen."

"Why?" I asked.

"Because I literally have no money. I am a student with a ton of debt. I'll never be in the position to do it."

"Actually," I said, "you can start right now. This moment."

I reached for a small stack of red paper coupons for free coffees sitting on the table. I placed them in her hand.

"I want you to hand these coupons out to random people today. You choose. Whomever you want. But the first step of a dream of being a philanthropist has nothing to do with money. It has everything to do with cultivating the kindness to give to others without asking for anything in return."

In the process of taking steps toward a life we crave, sometimes we just need a push to take the first step.

Your turn.

Scare Your Soul Challenge: Take Your First Small Step

Reflect on the dream you wrote about earlier in this chapter. Now, think of one small step that you could take in the next twenty-four hours that would move you (even minutely) toward that goal. Maybe it's a call or an email, or opening a blank document that will be the first page of a novel; maybe it's learning five words in Swahili for your dream trip to Tanzania.

Now, write it down and commit to doing it.

_____

_____

_____

_____

And five new words that describe how taking action makes you feel:

_____

_____

Claire Follows Her Bliss

I was tired of living in Los Angeles. I'd moved out to the big city from Memphis with stars in my eyes, to work in the music business. It was stimulating and thrilling, but after four years, LA lost its glitter. No matter where I looked, I saw cracks in the sidewalk.

I evaluated the course of my life. I kept thinking if I didn't make a change, I'd wake up one day to find myself with permanent roots in a place I didn't truly love. I was uninspired, tired, in need of serenity. Although it was a frightening admission, I knew I needed a new plan.

A sensitive friend addressed my discontent with a question: "If you could live anywhere, where would it be?"

Ireland was my answer. I imagined myself living in verdant fields partitioned by gray stone walls on the way to the sea, writing poetry. "There's only one way to do this," I said to my friend. "It starts with a leap of faith and a plane ticket."

It seemed once I'd made the decision to move to Ireland, the powers that be aligned in support, and uncanny things transpired. I received helpful information from surprising quarters, and it gave me a sense of being in tune with destiny.

I spent a year and a half living by the sea on the west coast of Ireland because I'd followed my bliss. I lived a life imagined with friends, a home, and a job with a business dedicated to the careers of Irish musicians. Every evening, I went home and documented the day in my journal.

The tides turned when I received a job offer in America and moved back to the States. Once there, I looked through my Irish journals and knew I had a great story about a young woman who'd moved to rural Ireland without a plan.

That story turned out to be the first of five novels. The courage to follow my bliss launched my writing career, and Ireland will be in my heart forever.

A Dream No Longer Deferred

To be nobody but yourself in a world which is doing its best, night and day, to make you everybody else—means to fight the hardest battle which any human being can fight; and never stop fighting. —E. E. CUMMINGS

At fifty-three, Johanna is wildly funny, irreverent, and bright. She has this otherworldly curly black hair and briliant blue eyes that squint into a mischievous wink when she tells a goofy joke.

Johanna grew up ensconced in LA's throbbing 1970s acting and art scene, the daughter of a prominent entertainment agent father and a teacher-and-writer mom. As soon as she could walk and talk, she was dancing and performing. She would spend weekends at the Directors Guild seeing movies and voraciously attended as much theater as possible. When Johanna graduated from high school, she entered the Groundlings Theatre & School, a famous center for improvisational comedy. In all ways, she loved performing and performers.

Always close with her father, she would watch Los Angeles Lakers' games with him. As he would cheer on the Lakers players, however, Johanna's attention was focused on another kind of performer.

She was fascinated by the cheerleaders.

She loved their enthusiasm and athleticism. She watched them, enraptured, memorizing their routines, delivering imaginary color commentaries in her head as they leapt and tumbled: *Oh, that was a great twisting double flip there! Yes, but her legs could have been straighter. Good point; there's some work to be done on the form, but all in all, a great routine so far.*

One day, she promised herself, she would be one of them.

• • •

When I first met Johanna twenty years later and after her relocation to the Midwest, she was living a life far from the lofty visions of her youth. Life, instead, felt to her like a cascading set of challenges.

She was now a divorced mom of three young children, reeling from a recent bout of lymphoma. The cancer was finally in remission, but the disease had left her tired and bewildered—and her day-to-day drained her further.

She was working as a nurse for a company that paired her with patients living in horrendous circumstances; she'd often use a portion of her modest salary to buy essentials for her patients. Despite the many responsibilities her own children required of her, she somehow found time to visit her patients in her rare hours off, making sure they were safe.

• • •

When I founded Scare Your Soul, Johanna loved the idea of taking action to battle fear. We talked about it, and she quickly asked if she could participate. "Of course," I said. "I just want you to find one thing that you NEED to do…something that will scare the hell out of you…and when you do it, it will unlock something that has been locked away for a long time."

She thought about it and then called me. She had an idea. "A really good one," she told me.

The next day, Johanna called the as-of-then-unknown athletic director at Shaker Heights High School, a large and well-known public school in Cleveland's eastern suburbs. She got his voicemail and left a message:

"Hello! You don't know me, but my name is Johanna. I am a mother, nurse, cancer survivor, and a participant in the Scare Your Soul courage movement. I have always wanted to be a cheerleader. And I am wondering if there is any way on God's green earth that you could help me make that happen. I can't even believe I am making this call right now, but if you think you can help, would you call me back?"

She hung up, feeling foolish. Until twenty minutes later, when he called back.

He absolutely loved the idea. He would speak to the head cheerleading coach and get back to her. Two days later, she received the call.

The coach—and every single one of the members of the Shaker Heights Raiders cheerleading squad—had voted unanimously. She would train with them for a full week, learn the cheers, and cheer with them at the stadium for the biggest game of the year. Johanna hung up and broke into tears of joy.

The next week was a blur of practices, learning routines, trial and error. But because of her background as a dancer and performer, she was a quick study. A lingering fear stuck in her mind, however. As she would tell me later, "I was really nervous about shoving my size sixteen body into a high school cheerleading uniform."

At the last practice, they handed Johanna that Raider cheerleading uniform. It fit perfectly.

The morning of the big game, Johanna found herself alone in the high school bathroom, pinning her curly hair back into a bun. As she looked at herself in the mirror, fear intruded. She suddenly felt ridiculous. "Who does this? What middle-aged nurse does something so silly?"

Her mind flashed forward, playing out lifelike scenarios where she was laughed off the field. Her kids would be ridiculed at school for their mom's antics. None of them would ever live down the shame.

Head down, she retreated from the bathroom and walked down the long hallway to the stadium.

As she and the squad jogged from the tunnel into the lights of Rupp Field, she looked at the other cheerleaders' slender bodies. She thought, *I can't turn back, but I can't move ahead!*

Fear was overtaking her.

In her ears, she heard the announcer say, "Ladies and gentlemen, give it up for your Shaker Raider cheerleaders!

"And joining them is special guest Johanna! Mother of three and a cancer survivor, Johanna is living out her dream of being a cheerleader here tonight!" Johanna and the squad ran across the infield and onto the side of the field. As they came to a halt, Johanna turned to face a crowd numbering in the hundreds.

A crowd that, person by person, stood to give her a standing ovation.

The cheer performance was a hit. Johanna loved every moment. A local news station was on hand and filmed it all, broadcasting her achievement. And when she sat in the stands afterward, there was a steady stream of adults who came to congratulate her. The superintendent had tears in his eyes. One woman in her fifties, misty with emotion, gave Johanna a hug, saying, "I have always wanted to do what you did but never had the bravery. Thank you for what you did. Thank you on behalf of all of us."

Johanna has a special photo that was taken that night.

It's a shot of her next to a tall, strapping football player in his uniform, grinning from ear to ear. He had asked politely if she would honor him by taking a photo standing by his side. She keeps that photo handy on her phone.

It reminds her that she is always one courageous act away from living a dream and inspiring others.

Key Insights

1. Dreams help to illuminate what we truly desire in our lives as well as what fuels that desire.

2. As we will see more dramatically later in the book, how our dreams make us *feel* is so important to understanding their power.

3. Langston Hughes, in his poem "Harlem," poses the question "What happens to a dream deferred?" Our recognition of the dreams that remain unattended to helps guide our direction toward an exceptional life.

CHAPTER 4

Designing Your Audacious Courage Manifesto

Success is not final, failure is not fatal: it is the courage to continue that counts. —WINSTON CHURCHILL

Congratulations! We've done it!

Well, you've done it, but I've been by your side the whole time.

You're on your way to taking active strides toward a more courageous life. Now it's time to put your stake in the ground, to declare your intent, passion, and commitment to leading a more courageous life.

What you need now is a manifesto. YES! Your own *courage manifesto*. One that will guide your efforts for the remainder of this book and beyond.

Think of this first section—"A Values-Driven Life"—as laying the foundation of a pyramid. There will be time to layer in more complex, nuanced ideas and goals, but for now, we want the firm grounding of who *you* are to form the basis for your manifesto.

For the purposes of this work, *values* are the core characteristics and motivators you hold in highest esteem. Values drive how we live and work. They determine priorities and, deep down, are the self-measure used to determine whether we're flourishing or floundering.

A Values-Driven Life

In this exercise, I'll help you identify your core values. First, here are two tips, articulated by Richard Boyatzis, Melvin L. Smith, and Ellen Van Oosten in their book *Helping People Change*,[1] to clarify this work:

1. Imagine how you would feel if you had to give up believing in or acting on a certain value.
2. How would you feel if your entire life revolved around that one value?

In what follows, I've listed a number of foundational values.

Circle your top ten (or add your own in the spaces provided). Afterward, we will whittle that list down. I'll work alongside you.

Accomplishment	Fun	Reliability
Adventure	Genuineness	Religiosity
Ambition	Happiness	Self-reliance
Care	Health	Sincerity
Charity	Honesty	Spirituality
Cheer	Hope	Success
Clarity	Imagination	Tenderness
Comfort	Innovation	Tranquility
Compassion	Joy	Transformation
Competency	Kindness	Wealth
Connection	Logic	Wisdom
Courage	Love	_____
Creativity	Maturity	_____
Effectiveness	Peace	_____
Fame	Power	_____
Forgiveness	Rationality	_____

There is real power and clarity when we engage in physically writing our thoughts and realizations, so even though you've circled them, write them down here:

1. _____

2. _____

3. _____

4. _____

5. _____

6. _____

7. _____

8. _____

9. _____

10. _____

Mine are *adventure, compassion, connection, creativity, genuineness, imagination, joy, love, sincerity,* and *transformation.*

Now, take your list and, of the ten values you selected, narrow them down to a top five. Which ones constitute the core of *your* life?

Next to your choices, write out why you chose them.

For example, my five primary core values are these:

Compassion—how I ideally want to view and treat others

Connection—my main strength and how I want to serve the world professionally

Joy—my happiest state of being and one that I desire the most

Love—how I feel when I care deeply for others

Transformation—the passion I have deep inside to impact the world

Now, it's all you:

1. _____

2. _____

3. _____

4. _____

5. _____

The Two Wheels: Excitement and Fear

Now you'll find two charts: the Wheel of Excitement and the Wheel of Fear. Coaches, psychologists, and researchers have used similar constructs for years as indicators of how we define certain areas of our lives. The charts will aid you in illuminating where your excitement lives and where your fear is most present.

The Wheel of Excitement

The Wheel of Excitement is an opportunity for you to get in touch with where your own sense of energy and delight connects with Scare Your Soul's Seven Principles: gratitude, adventure, energy, curiosity, awe, forgiveness, and work.

Take time to rank each category and plot it on the wheel that follows. Something to consider as you rank is this: *Right now, here is how excited I am about this particular endeavor.* The number 1 represents no excitement at all; 10 means "I'm jumping out of my seat to pursue this."

_____ *Awe*—how excited are you to see the spiritual side of life, to seek out transcendent experiences that fill you with appreciation for the world, nature, and the connectedness of humanity?

_____ *Curiosity*—how excited are you to maintain a curious attitude toward the world, to learn passionately about others, pursue intellectual growth, and connect deeply with love?

_____ *Energy*—how excited are you to focus on the mind/body connection, to energize your body and keep your mind sharp and alive?

_____ *Gratitude*—how excited are you to practice appreciation in real and meaningful ways, to feel grateful for your own life and be able to express that thankfulness?

_____ *Forgiveness*—how excited are you to learn how to free yourself from the bitterness and hurt that hold you back?

_____ *Adventure*—how excited are you to see life as an unfolding journey full of mystery?

_____ *Work*—how excited are you to work in a way that fulfills your passions, to reinvent yourself without fear of disappointing others, and to generate ideas and concepts that will let your work life skyrocket?

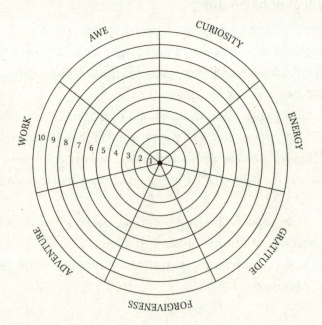

Great! List the top five areas that received your highest rankings:

1. _____

2. _____

3. _____

4. _____

5. _____

The Wheel of Fear

This exercise will help you understand which fears are blocking you the most now from leading your most powerful, positive life. This isn't about judging; it's about accepting which fears lie deepest within you. Through the identification of fears, we'll harness power over them (much more to come on that in chapter 5).

As you did with the last exercise, take time to rank each of the following categories. Think about this when you rank: *At this moment, here is how powerful this fear feels to me.* The number 1 represents no fear at all; 10 means "this really, really freaks me out."

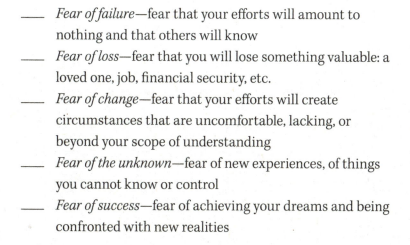

____ *Fear of failure*—fear that your efforts will amount to nothing and that others will know

____ *Fear of loss*—fear that you will lose something valuable: a loved one, job, financial security, etc.

____ *Fear of change*—fear that your efforts will create circumstances that are uncomfortable, lacking, or beyond your scope of understanding

____ *Fear of the unknown*—fear of new experiences, of things you cannot know or control

____ *Fear of success*—fear of achieving your dreams and being confronted with new realities

_____ *Fear of rejection*—fear of asking for something of value or meaning and being told no

_____ *Fear of not being good enough*—fear of a negative comparison between you and others, as in not being smart enough, successful enough, thin enough, etc.

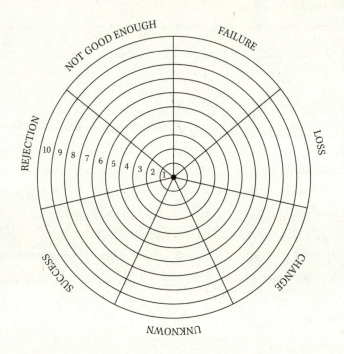

As before, list the top five areas that received the highest (the greatest level of fear) rankings:

1. _____

2. _____

3. _____

4. _____

5. _____

Liz Starts a New Life

The last thing I remember about my 2:30 a.m. departure is that I felt so glad it was the final day of the horse show. I was finally looking forward to an actual full night of sleep! Then it happened.

The next thing I remember is wondering where I was. And why I was strapped to a bed.

I was in the ICU.

A stranger had found me, unconscious in my severely mangled car, only a hundred yards from the barn's driveway.

My injuries were catastrophic, my doctors would report to my family. My survival was touch and go for several days. It was a deeply frightening time for my family and friends as they struggled with not knowing whether I would survive, and if so, whether I might need care for the rest of my life.

But I did survive. And surviving meant the beginning of a new journey.

And as my healing commenced, the stark understanding of my new life began to unfold.

I had suffered a traumatic brain injury, and the effects were staggering. I was thirty-two years old but had reverted to an eight-year-old in behavior, speech, and dependency. I could read but not understand the words. I could recognize pictures of items but not remember what to call them. I was dizzy and tired, unable to stand up straight or walk in a straight line. I didn't know how to dial a phone and incessantly repeated myself.

And deep inside, I was experiencing a level of fear I had never experienced.

Looking back now, I realize I began a new life that early morning of 1998.

I became a different person. A more thankful one. I am not embarrassed by my brain injury or feeling the least bit "stupid" or "incapable." Instead, I feel so appreciative of my ability to smile, walk, talk, and be wonderfully alive! I am forever grateful for my strong recovery.

I will always be faced with daily challenges that go unnoticed by others. They are all too clear to me. Yet these challenges are what fuel me to push past fear and accomplish whatever it is I set my mind to achieve.

I am always living in the moment because I know well how, in a blink of an eye, it can be taken away forever. Fear can take a backseat.

I am all about my brand of courageous living.

Your Best Possible Self

Now that we have clarified our core values, excitements, and fears, we can look ahead to our future and create powerful commitments from a more nuanced and knowledgeable place of who we really are.

In 2000, Professor Laura King and her colleagues at Southern Methodist University gave a simple set of writing instructions to eighty-one undergraduates in an effort to understand the positive impact of recording life goals. The impact this had on the students was dramatic: overall, they experienced better physical health five months afterward, cementing this simple and powerful exercise as an important one in the practice of positive psychology.

In this case, we will do the exercise once and distill its essential elements. (You can, of course, do it multiple times if you wish.) So, grab a journal or several sheets of paper (I suggest that you do this longhand rather than on a computer or phone, if possible).

In your journal, answer Laura King's famous exercise:

Take a moment to imagine your life in the future. What is the best possible life you can imagine? Consider all of the relevant areas of your life, such as your career, academic work, relationships, hobbies, and health. What would happen in these areas of your life in your best possible future? For the next 15 minutes, write continuously about what you imagine this best possible future to be.[2]

A few quick tips as you do it:

- Don't judge your writing. There are no right or wrong answers.
- Try to tune out the voice that says, *What will others think?*
- Try to get specific into the details of your best possible future. What are you doing? What do you see? How do you feel?

Now, your final task before your Audacious Courage Manifesto comes together is this: read your Best Possible Self essay again.

This time, *read it out loud*. Pay attention to how you feel when you read your own vision for an ideal future.

Now, choose three words that describe how you felt when you read it.

Mine were *excited*, *inspired*, and *motivated*.

1. _____

2. _____

3. _____

Now you are ready to complete your Audacious Courage Manifesto. Keep it and your Best Possible Self exercise close to you, as you will want to refer to them throughout your work ahead.

Your Audacious Courage Manifesto

I, _____ , do hereby on this day,

_____ , make the following commitments:

I. I commit to living a life that is grounded in my five most deeply held values: _____ , _____ ,

_____ , _____ , and _____ .

(Fill in from "A Values-Driven Life" section.)

II. I will continue to live in my power, drawing strength from pursuing the areas that feel the most exciting: _____ ,

_____ , _____ , _____ , and

_____ . (Fill in from "The Wheel of Excitement" section.)

III. I commit to being vitally aware of the five top fears that I have the greatest opportunity of overcoming: _____ ,

_____ , _____ , _____ , and

_____ . (Fill in from "The Wheel of Fear" section.)

IV. Finally, I have an ideal life and I see it clearly. It is my vision for where my courageous action will take me. My vision is

_____ , _____ , and _____ .

(Fill in from "Your Best Possible Self" section.)

Signed, _____

PART II

Diving Deeper

Harnessing Fear, Flight, and Failure

CHAPTER 5

Harnessing Our Fears

The cave you fear to enter holds the treasure you seek.

—JOSEPH CAMPBELL

A quick Google search of "how to be fearless" yields more than 105,000,000 results. A similar search for books on the subject of fearlessness yields over 8,000,000. Our society has adopted an endless—bordering on militaristic—fascination with "overcoming"... "conquering"..."destroying" the fears that we all experience every day.

I suggest the following: *ignore it all.*

Fear is an inextricable part of being human. Instead of eradicating it (which, for normal, functioning *Homo sapiens*, is impractical and dangerous, if not impossible), I invite you to consider another path altogether:

Harness your fears. Get to know them. *Dance with them.*

It sounds counterintuitive, I know.

The truth is, even though I engage in courage work every single day, I am fearful, too. I fear a never-ending carnival ride of fears: fear of failing at things I care about, of being ostracized, of disappointing others. I am fearful of losing people I love, of regressing, of getting old, of being rejected or irrelevant, of not reaching my potential.

Many of our fears—whether we are conscious of them or not—are born from intense past experiences. These traumas have a significant impact on our emotional landscape. Intense experiences of negative emotion are a wake-up call for our brain centers, wiring those experiences deep into the memory centers of our brains.

Sometimes, we have the time and space to gain power and actively tackle our fears (as I did in my public singing experiment).

And sometimes, we literally have no choice at all. A crisis arrives, and we have no choice but to rely on the courage-muscle that we have worked hard to develop. We are presented with the deep fear inherent in those moments, when we say "this can't be happening."

"This Can't Be Happening"

The most important decision we make is whether we believe in a friendly or hostile universe. —ALBERT EINSTEIN

During the days following my divorce, I moved to a small apartment miles away from home. I had the kids 50 percent of the time, and the hours without them felt interminably long and sad. On my "off-nights," I would come home from work and nearly double over when I saw their action figures and American Girl dolls on the living room floor.

So I made a commitment: When I did have the kids with me, I would welcome their friends over any time. There would be an open door policy. Somehow, making platters of tacos and pizza for their friends made that once-lonely apartment come alive.

When I finally was able to move into a house, the kitchen became the meeting spot. Friday nights were especially busy there, and I thought of it as my own buzzing Grand Central Station.

I loved it all: the flurry of kids arriving and departing, the laughter, the surreptitious Snapchat scrolling (like I wasn't noticing), footballs tossed high over kids cartwheeling across the cold front-yard grass.

One of those cartwheelers one particular Friday night was my daughter's friend Sophie. A born entertainer, at thirteen she was happy, energetic, and funny beyond words. I loved that her parents and the parents of so many others trusted me to keep their kids happy and safe. And safety was of paramount importance to me... especially when it came to one issue: crossing streets.

My fear was deeply rooted in one of my own past traumas.

When I was just a shade younger than Sophie, my hero, my idol, my older first cousin Steven was struck by a car and killed crossing a street at age fourteen. I remember his funeral: the tears, the numbness, the stark disbelief. I will never forget watching a packet of smelling salts being passed around to those on the verge of fainting.

From that day forward, I succumbed to a powerful fear of crossing streets. I would look both ways a dozen times when pulling out of a simple parking lot in my car. And when it came to kids crossing streets, the fear was nearly debilitating.

Little did I know that a cool Friday evening would test my ability to cope with that fear like never before.

• • •

I was at my kitchen sink, hands deep in the soapy dinner dishes, when I heard the first scream outside. Fear grabbed hold of me instantly.

Within seconds, I had sprinted through the front door, barefoot across the chilly, wet grass. I felt the sting of gravel on my heels as I made a hard left, directly into the busy street that adjoined our quiet one. Sophie was sprawled in the middle of the road.

She and one friend had very innocently chosen to leave the confines of my yard to explore, crossing a busy street to get there. Darting back, one made it. Sophie didn't. She was hit by an oncoming SUV.

I have never felt such intense fear in my entire life.

Something inside propelled me forward. I ran toward Sophie, stepped over her, and stretched my arms out wide toward the oncoming traffic. The soul-crushing fear rose higher in me as I did everything in my power to do what I didn't want to do: I looked down. Sophie was still as a stone.

Oh my God, no! No! This can't be happening! Again!

I gazed back up at the headlights coming from both directions.

Heart beating through my chest, I decided to take one—just one—long breath. I had lost Steven. I was going to protect Sophie.

I said to myself, "OK, this is happening. You're going to handle this. Stay put. Get the kids back in the house, and then stand your ground for as long as it takes. Do it. *Now!*"

As quickly as the sensations had drained from my body, they returned. I felt my toes on the cold street. I shouted orders to the kids now huddled, crying, on the curb.

"Get inside NOW! Call 911!"

And there I stood. Hands outstretched. Praying for Sophie's life. And not budging an inch.

. . .

We spent the evening in the emergency room. When her injuries were deemed too serious, Sophie was taken by ambulance to a larger hospital. She survived the night.

When I saw her parents—my dear friends—the following morning, we collapsed into each other's arms. I told them how terribly sorry I was. This had happened on my watch, after all. They assured me that it was all OK. They thanked me. We hugged tighter.

Just weeks later, after a team of doctors and nurses at the Cleveland Clinic expertly tended to her broken bones and bruised organs, Sophie proudly walked back into her eighth-grade classroom. Six weeks after the accident, she was on her way with the school's class trip to Israel.

I am proud to report that, as of this writing, Sophie is a happy, vibrant college sophomore. Yes, she still has an unmistakable glint of adventure in her eye. And yes, she and I will forever be connected.

And through it all, standing in the fire of fear in the most awful of situations, I was myself released from the noose of my past trauma.

I didn't want it or ask for it, but coming face-to-face with one of the worst fears imaginable—the loss of a precious life in the street—and not backing down changed me.

Now, the fear of crossing a street, while still present, holds so much less power over me.

Sophie was healed; and I was freed.

Writing Prompt: Memories That Protect and Memories That Are Dangerous

Harvard psychiatry professor and prolific researcher Kerry Ressler writes extensively about the power of memory, and how memories can either be protective or dangerous. When memories are protective, they guard us against similar future events that might hurt us, physically or emotionally. When memories are dangerous, one bad experience can result in debilitating fear.

A question: Can you think of a time when something scary or traumatic happened to you, and you learned a lesson that protects you now?

_____

_____

_____

Now, can you think of a time when something scary or traumatic happened to you, and the trauma of the experience—and the fear because of it—has held you back from progressing in your life?

_____

_____

_____

The Fear Response

Fear is only as deep as the mind allows.

—JAPANESE PROVERB

I invite you to picture three scenes:

One day you're walking by yourself in the woods. You're feeling the calm wind on your face, and then you hear a branch snap. You stop, looking into the brush. Then, in an instant, out of the thicket comes a full-size black bear. He's charging right at you.

Now, this:

You've always hated heights, which is why you can't believe you agreed to go skydiving. Now you are all suited up and strapped to a tandem partner who you only met thirty minutes ago and who smells suspiciously like day-old weed. The door to the Cessna slides open. You *scooch* toward it, looking downward at fourteen thousand feet of empty space below you. Your partner leans in and yells amidst the deafening wind, "Time to jump!"

Finally, this:

You're at the mall, shopping for your friend's big birthday party on Saturday night. It's going to be a huge crowd. Just then, you see your friend's husband, who says, "I am so glad you are coming to Jane's birthday party this weekend! By the way, I would love everyone to stand up and share a few stories about her." All you can think about is that embarrassing time you froze up when giving a speech as a teenager and how you've despised public speaking ever since. Then he adds, "Oh, and I would love for you to go first to make everyone else feel comfortable!"

All three situations—totally different—would provoke some sort of a fearful reaction, right? But are the reactions the same in our brains and in our bodies? And what can we learn about fear that will help us in these situations?

What is this complicated dance we do with fear?

Getting under the Hood

To really begin the process of harnessing our fear, it's important to understand what it is and how it works in our bodies. For some this is old news, and for others it may seem wonky, but let's get under the hood and see what's really going on.

Our brains contain an incredibly intricate circuit of specialized cells that process threatening stimuli and coordinate our "fear response."

That response originates in a region of the brain called the amygdala—"almond" in Greek—which is, not surprisingly, an almond-shaped part of our brain dedicated to detecting the nature of all forms of stimuli. The amygdala is constantly taking in all types of sensations (including smells in a restaurant and the facial expression of the stranger walking toward us on the street), and when sensing a threat, it directs a nearly instantaneous set of coordinated events.

Its first distress signal engages another brain structure, the hypothalamus, which then sends chemical messages to our adrenal glands, which sit at the top of our kidneys. They dump hormones into our system, kicking off immediate physiological changes: our heart and breathing rates increase, our sight and hearing get notably sharper, and blood sugar and fat stores are released into our veins to provide more energy to our body (just to name a few).

Incredibly, all of this activity happens so quickly that we often aren't even consciously aware of the stimuli when the chain of reactions begins. Our processing center—the prefrontal cortex—is just getting around to that important work.

As the initial surge of epinephrine subsides, the hypothalamus activates the second component of the stress response system—known as the HPA (hypothalamus, pituitary, adrenal) axis. This network relies on a series of hormonal signals to keep the sympathetic nervous system—the "gas pedal"—pressed down. If the brain continues to perceive something as dangerous, the hypothalamus releases corticotropin-releasing hormone, which travels to the pituitary gland, triggering the release of adrenocorticotropic hormone. The adrenal glands release more chemicals, including cortisol, the body's main stress hormone.

If our brain perceives that the threat has passed, the cortisol levels in our blood are detected, and through a process called the negative feedback loop, the cortisol level is reduced. Only then do we begin to calm down.

Just one stimulus—the charging bear, the view from a Cessna doorway, even the thought of public speaking—can kick off this massive set of reactions within us.

It's no wonder that fear keeps us wanting to hide safely in our comfort zones.

The Scalpel and the Butter Knife

> Your brain issues motor predictions to move your body well before you become aware of your intent to move.
>
> —DR. LISA FELDMAN BARRETT

In the face of a true threat—like a runaway car speeding toward you—it's actually good news that our amygdala has a direct line to the adrenals without first going to our neocortex. We don't have time to think, *Hey, that Volkswagen is coming at me pretty fast!* Instead, we dive out of the way to safety.

But the amygdala, in its haste to act quickly, can be a blunt tool. It is well suited for threat response but not for well-thought-out interpretation of a threat. In that regard, think of it as a surgeon holding a butter knife rather than a scalpel.

Or think of it another way: You're visiting a haunted house. As you walk the dark, creepy hallways, you surely know that the potential "threats" around you are not real (you chose to pay the ten-dollar entrance fee, after all). But when a clown with a blood-curdling scream suddenly pops up in front of you, you yell, your body flies backward, and your heart beats full tilt...all before you can process the fact that the clown is actually your friend Brian who loves hanging out at haunted houses.

The amygdala and other brain processes are attuned to experiences from our past and to concepts that our brain creates to understand the world around us. On that one afternoon when we are badly stung by a yellow jacket, our brains construct the association *wasp = pain*. The next time one lands on our cheek, you better believe that we will react.

SaraMarie Confronts a Fear

Most people would describe me as nearly fearless.

I carry a free spirit and positive energy into most experiences. So it was surprising to not only me, but everyone around me, that when it came to showing affection to others, I was gripped with fear. I would watch others walking hand in hand down the street and feel a pit of anxiety in my stomach. How are they able to be so vulnerable?

I didn't recognize that this fear was holding me back in any way; I simply avoided any situation where someone might try to hold my hand.

However, when asked, "What's your biggest fear?" I immediately blurted out, "Holding hands in public!" Even I was shocked by this ludicrous answer, but the mere mention caused my heart to race.

I experienced abuse in my childhood. I grew up very guarded, never allowing people too close.

I also grew up with a strong motivation to achieve high levels of excellence. So, for those around me, I was outgoing, energetic, a leader, and maybe a little intimidating. It's not that I didn't want to hold hands; I just couldn't do it. So I enrolled my friend to support me in setting out to change this.

We met at the mall, and I explained to him that we were going to walk around holding hands for at least five minutes.

I almost backed out, but I took a breath and grabbed his hand. After the first minute of anxiety passed, I felt myself crack open. The part of me that truly desired this affection was overwhelmed with joy. It was a scary moment of my fear facing my joy and recognizing that I hold the power to choose which side I stand on.

I must admit that there are days I still feel fear, but I'm quickly reminded of the joy from this day and I find my courage again. Today, I hold hands, I hug, and I allow myself to flow with ease when showing physical affection. This practice has brought me love and peace and fulfilled a part of my life that I didn't know I needed.

Rewiring Our Associations

Our minds have the incredible capacity to both alter the strength of connections among neurons, essentially rewiring them, and create entirely new pathways. (It makes a computer, which cannot create new hardware when its system crashes, seem fixed and helpless.) —SUSANNAH CALAHAN

As you no doubt already know, we ourselves have an active role to play in changing how our own brains operate.

At one time, scientists thought that our brains were essentially "locked in" after childhood. Although researchers and psychologists like Ivan Pavlov in the early 1900s proved that our brains and behaviors could change, more recent imaging and other techniques reveal that our brains are even more malleable and adaptable than ever thought before. Through the study of that process—called neuroplasticity—we can actually play a very active role in rewiring our own brains.

Critical to that process is the creation of new associations—taking formerly traumatic, scary, or fearful experiences and mapping new ones. Our Scare Your Soul model is a hybrid of a number of approaches and is both user-friendly and effective: a sequential process of naming or labeling our fear, accepting its existence, reducing the anxiety around it, determining whether or not it should be heeded, taking action, and then actively working to rewrite our past internal stories and rewiring our brain's associations. The model is called the LADDER:

Labeling and writing
Acceptance and permission
De-energizing and de-escalating
Determination and judgment
Effort and action
Rewriting and rewiring

Climbing the LADDER

Let's take this opportunity to get familiar with the LADDER.

Labeling and Writing

There is a palpable sense of authority and ownership when we give a name to something we are feeling. Psychologist Dan Siegel refers to this practice as "name it to tame it."[1] Left to their own devices, our emotions can feel overwhelming. But research has shown that mere verbal (or written) labeling of fear can help us gain control over it. fMRI brain scans reveal that labeling decreases activity in the brain's emotional centers, especially the amygdala.[2]

This action allows our frontal lobe to help us process the stimulus. So, imagine a large, blank whiteboard in front of you on which you get to label your fear in red marker. Imagine the action that is causing the fear, and ask yourself the question *How am I really feeling?*

Take some time and let the emotion arise. Then write it out. Maybe it's "I am feeling afraid of failing in front of others." Or, "I'm anxious about embarrassing myself and having people ridicule me."

Literally writing out our feelings kicks off the process of us taking control.

Acceptance and Permission

Once our fear has a label, we can begin to investigate it.

Ask yourself—kindly and without judgment—why this feeling is arising. Where is it coming from? Maybe there was a past trauma or painful experience that generated it. Maybe it stems from responsibilities that we have to others or ourselves. Maybe it is rooted in fear of adverse implications if our action goes awry.

Regardless, allow yourself the grace to experience this emotion, even if it stings. You're human and you are engaging in one of the most courageous human exercises: sitting with fear and not budging.

De-energizing and De-escalating

Mindfulness plays a role here. First, I invite you to sit with the feeling. Let it be, in all its intensity, and just abide.

Imagine your life as if this fear has evaporated and you no longer had to carry its burden. And then ask yourself, *What would it feel like to not possess this fear at all?*

Life might feel different. You might make other choices or take other actions, right? Let yourself begin to feel the anxious energy dissipate as you consider a life without this fear. Like toggling a circuit breaker in an electrical panel, reduce the voltage if you can.

Determination and Judgment

Now we bring our prefrontal cortex to the stage as we process the truth about this fear. Is the fear serving us? Protecting us? Stopping us from something that would help us grow and come alive?

Let's work to simplify the emotion so we can judge it. Let's think about fear in the context of "true fears" and "false fears." In her book *The Fear Cure*, Dr. Lissa Rankin writes that "true fear" is that automatic and appropriate response to something that could endanger us or others around us. "False fear," on the other hand, is a product of our minds that doesn't relate to safety but instead points to an area of growth and healing:

> True fear is what you experience when your minivan goes out of control on the interstate. False fear, on the other hand, shows up as worry, anxiety, rumination about all of the things that could go wrong in an imaginary future. It's always the finger pointing toward something that needs to be healed in your mind. In this way, true fear and false fear can help you, if you know how to interpret them in healthy ways.[3]

Now that you've named the fear, accepted its validity, and reduced its intensity, ask yourself these questions:

- *Is the fear rational or irrational?*
- *Is the fear something that is keeping me safe, or is it holding me back from what I need to do?*
- *Could the fear be possibly alerting me that this is a growth opportunity?*

It's here that we make our determination. Step back or move forward?

If it's time to step toward a fear, we move into effort and action.

Effort and Action

Carol Dweck, famed American psychologist, author, researcher, and Stanford University professor, first developed the idea of "fixed" and "growth" mindsets; in short, she suggests that much of our human potential is based on our belief about whether we can actually change.

In her book *Mindset*, Dweck writes, "Effort is one of the things that gives meaning to life. Effort means you care about something, that something is important to you and you are willing to work for it. It would be an impoverished existence if you were not willing to value things and commit yourself to working toward them."[4]

Effort is rooted in the word *esfort*, or Old French for "strength or might." So, follow me here—our Scare Your Soul reading of Dweck's mindsets is all about (you guessed it!) harnessing fear by being brave enough to put fear into practice and learn from it.

Taking action is the ultimate form of stepping forward with strength into the void, into the uncertainty that is guarded by fear. Say to yourself, "I can do this."

And then do it.

Rewriting and Rewiring

The key to rewiring our neural pathways is in the explicit mental effort we take in "rewriting" a past trauma or negative association with a new, positive one.

After you have taken the effort to act in the face of fear, take time to process the experience. Maybe you feel great; if so, remind yourself that you accomplished something that previously had a negative association, and tackling it was actually a hell of a lot of fun! Let it really sink in.

If the experience didn't end the way you had wished, remind yourself that you are courageous for taking action anyway and that you have "agency" in your own life and won't let fears hold you back.

Regardless, explicitly re-telling the new story is critical to the process of rewiring. Your old, negative story is now a positive—or at least a courageous—one.

Scare Your Soul Challenge: Climbing the LADDER

Let's experiment. I invite you to think about a fear that you believe is holding you back from something in your life that feels relevant right now: Maybe you are putting something off because you're afraid, or you've chosen to be in denial that it even exists. Yes, that one.

Now, let's put this into action:

1. Labeling and writing

Write out the fear here, including how it makes you feel when you experience it.

_____

_____

2. Acceptance and permission

Take a moment to search back to understand why you are having this fear. Does the action feel unsafe? Does it bring up feelings connected to past events? Actively give yourself permission to feel these very human feelings. When you feel complete, move on.

3. De-energizing and de-escalating

Engage in the mental exercise of asking yourself, *How would my life feel if I didn't have this fear at all? If it somehow evaporated?* Really imagine that scenario. Do you feel a sense of relief? Something else? Actively allow yourself to reduce the intensity of this fear if you can.

4. Determination and judgment

Bring your sense of clear judgment to bear: Is fear legitimately protecting you from something dangerous to yourself or others? The answer may be yes! But if not, is there a chance that if you took action despite the fear, something positive (or even great) could happen? Are you willing to boldly take that risk? If so, move forward.

5. Effort and action

Here is where the rubber hits the road. Take action! Remind yourself that the outcome is not the goal; the very fact that you are making an effort to grow is considered success here.

6. Rewriting and rewiring

You did the thing that is going to light up your way: you took action despite fear. Now, don't let it pass by unrecognized. Remind yourself of the label, why that fear existed in the first place, how you—with clear eyes—took action. If the experience was positive, revel in that! If it wasn't (or it was neutral), remind yourself that small acts of courage define who you are now. One act will lead to more. And that leads to living an exceptional life.

You did it!

Take a moment or two to reflect on this experience. How did it impact you? Was it helpful? Can you imagine its impact growing as you practice it more consistently? How would your life change?

_____

_____

_____

While one way to begin overcoming a fear stemming from a past experience is by taking bold action, sometimes we need support from a trained therapist or psychologist to face some of our deeper traumas. There are great tools and resources to assist with that, such as eye movement desensitization and reprocessing (EMDR), internal family systems, Somatic Experiencing, and breathwork, just to name a few. This is a healing process and can take time to unfold. And, of course, enlisting support and taking the time and effort to heal take immense courage.

Let's Have Tea

The only way to ease our fear and be truly happy is to acknowledge our fear and look deeply at its source.

—THICH NHAT HANH

Twenty-six hundred years ago, Buddha, known then as Siddhartha Gautama, sat under the heart-shaped leaves of a bodhi tree the evening before his enlightenment.

Mara, a celestial demon-god, the god of the shadow side—often associated with fear and temptation—attacks him. Mara is desparate to keep Siddhartha Gautama from achieving enlightenment and, to do so, creates all kinds of apparitions meant to scare, tempt, and anger Siddhartha.

Having failed, Mara leaves.

But he will be back.

Again and again, Mara arrives in hopes of inculcating fear and temptation.

The Buddha has a loyal attendant, Ananda, who is always on the lookout for any harm that might come to his teacher. One day, agitated, he reports with dismay that Mara has again returned.

But this time, Buddha stops Ananda.

To Mara, he says, "Mara, I see you. Let's have tea."

Dear reader, I invite you to consider this: *How often do you invite fear in? How often do you sit and wait to hear what it has to say?*

Just like Mara's constant, consistent, and unwelcome visits, fear will always arrive on your doorstep. When you ignore it, you fall open to the danger fear is meant to protect; unheeded, it can upend a fulfilling life.

But when you actually acknowledge fear ("I see you") and befriend it ("Let's have tea"), you harness its immense power.

Key Insights

1. Traumas have a significant impact on how we process our current life and the fears we experience. But we do have opportunities to address them. Sometimes we choose to do so, and sometimes we have no choice. But it is here that we gain the power to harness fear.

2. Fear oftentimes presents itself in different ways—immediate situations, rumination about the future, connection to past events through association—but in most scenarios, our bodies don't discern the difference. Essential to harnessing fear is understanding the fear response.

3. Many of us love fear for the thrill that it gives us. The huge wave that we surf, the roller coaster we ride, the haunted house we visit. Because the experiences have a perception of control ("I know how to do this...I will be OK"; "It will be over soon"; "It's just a haunted house, so I can suspend disbelief for a while"), we can enjoy the bursts of adrenaline and dopamine without actually confronting the crazed killer with a pickaxe.

4. Our limbic system is a complex, well-coordinated set of body systems that are central to our fear response. The HPA axis is central to the quick actions that occur when we encounter a stimulus, oftentimes outpacing our own cognitive ability to process and understand a threat.

5. We can change our own brains. Research into neuroplasticity confirms that our brains are malleable and that we can rewire new pathways through specific actions. One of them is the action to push through fears so that we can create new positive associations. A template—LADDER—is one avenue for holistically harnessing fear and working toward rewriting our fear stories and rewiring our brains.

CHAPTER 6

Removing Before Flight

Don't be ashamed in needing help.

—MARCUS AURELIUS

It's late in the afternoon and you've been at the airport for hours now.

Your flight has been delayed twice, you now know concourse B as well as your own living room, and you've licked clean all of the salt from the bottom of your bag of pretzels.

Dreamily, you look out your gate's window at your 747, that honored chariot that soon—you hope—will spirit you home. Luckily, some action starts buzzing around the plane. Finally, you think. A catering truck pulls up. Saviors clad in gloves and earmuffs arrive and, with ease, swarm the jet's mechanicals.

Watching them in action, you see them remove large red tags that were previously hanging from the fuselage and wheels. You lean in, nose nearly pressed against the glass. There are words emblazoned in bold letters on the bright-red tags: REMOVE BEFORE FLIGHT.

As any pilot knows, these tags are an important aspect of getting a plane ready to fly. These tags are so revered among the flight community that enthusiasts have been known to showcase replicas of the tags on tchotchkes like key chains, lighters, and T-shirts.

Each red tag is attached to a single item—either a protective cover

63

or a pin on anything from a small tube to an entire jet engine. The tag alerts the mechanics that the cover or pin needs to be removed before the plane can leave its gate. They are signals that, to get airborne, the smallest preparatory acts will ensure the safety of a 350-ton Boeing hurtling at 600 miles per hour toward your hometown.

In a way, these bright red tags are what make the entire journey possible.

Throughout this book, I will continue to invite you to do things that scare you. They may make you want to retreat, rationalize, avoid, or feel like you're not capable.

The small acts—hacks, if you will—presented in this chapter will help you in moments when you need a boost, when you are feeling unsteady.

Pick and choose from the concepts that are most meaningful to you. Keep them in your mental toolbox for the times when you're tempted to give up or give in.

Red Tag #1: "I Avoid the Things That Make Me Uncomfortable"

You may delay, but time will not. —BENJAMIN FRANKLIN

I have an admission.

Writing a book…sitting and writing these words *right now*… feels nothing short of terrifying. To be more accurate, as a writer, I experience these lovely, small moments of joy and confidence, which only serve to briefly penetrate the deep well of fear. And I come rightly by my fears:

- I want this book to help you positively transform your life, but I'm afraid it won't connect with you.
- I want this book to change how people hold fear, but I'm afraid that they won't act on the challenges and make positive progress.

- I want this book to sit proudly on my local bookstore's shelf for years to come but am afraid it might not connect with an audience.
- I want to make my family, friends, mentors, teachers, editor, and first-grade teacher proud, but I am afraid of disappointing them all.

My fears make sense, right? The question is this: What do I do about them?

First, I have to overcome the myriad excuses I will no doubt create to stave off the challenging feelings. For example, in writing this chapter, I took notice of my own actions.

They are not flattering.

First, I got everything ready: Laptop plugged in? Check. Coffee brewed? Check. My notes from yesterday's brainstorming next to me for easy access? Check. Spotify writing playlist on? Check. And then I saw it. The lone cursor on my laptop screen, blinking...no, *taunting*. My heart began to pound, and the familiar, queasy feeling of dread started to creep up within me.

All of a sudden, it seemed monumentally important to:

- Reorganize the folders on my Google Drive (*I can't work if I'm not organized.*)
- Color-code the folders (*I work more efficiently when everything looks well designed.*)
- Change the room's temperature (*It's way too hot in here to write.*)
- Change that burnt-out light bulb in the bathroom (*I'll just do it quickly, so I don't forget.*)
- Get more coffee (*I'm down to half a cup, so I'd better get more now.*)
- Watch a quick YouTube video on making espresso in Italy (*I just find it so fascinating.*)

Any of this sound familiar?

Rationalize. Procrastinate. Rationalize. Procrastinate. And repeat.

Avoiding what we need to do because we are scared and uncertain of the outcome is both normal and insidious. As author and researcher Adam Grant says, "What causes procrastination is not the desire to avoid work. It's the desire to avoid feelings."[1]

But here's a deeper truth: *The fear we feel is directly proportional to the importance of the act we are trying to avoid.*

The more something means to your life, the more fear will try to deter you. And even well-established professionals suffer. Margaret Atwood is a prolific author; at the time of this writing, she has published eighteen books of poetry, eighteen novels (including *The Handmaid's Tale*), eleven books of nonfiction, nine collections of short fiction, eight children's books, and two graphic novels. But she put off writing for years. She would pad through her house all morning, full of stress and anxiety, making excuses.

She confessed that, to finally confront the fear around tackling her work, she had to create a mental hack. "I had another name that I grew up with and that gave me two names, so I had a double identity. So, Margaret does the writing and the other one [Peggy] does everything else."[2]

We all have different sides to our personalities, and by naming and calling forth the ones we want in any given circumstance, we bring out our qualities that matter most in the moment.

It's not fake. It's not pretending. And it works.

Tag-Removal Strategy: Choose Your Double Identity

Back in the day, an avatar was commonly understood as a divine teacher or a deity living on earth in bodily form. But these days, we know them more as cartoon-like icons that represent us on our phones, in chats, and video games. They highlight our most emblematic aspects: our looks, personality, and characteristics.

You probably already have an avatar of yourself, but what would your *courage* avatar look like?

What do you look and sound like when you are most courageous? A superhero? Someone from a movie or book you love? A tiger? A volcano?

Insight Exercise: Create Your Own Courage Avatar

Use the following space to draw what your avatar looks like. Have fun. Be creative. Surround your drawing with five words that describe your courage qualities.

Red Tag #2: "I Can't Get Past My Anxiety"

> You cannot always control what goes on outside, but you
> can always control what goes on inside. —WAYNE DYER

When we are confronted with a new and challenging task, we all, in some way, experience some sense of anxiety. My hands get clammy and my heart rate quickens, but I really feel butterflies in my gut. What happens to you?

Over the years, researchers have developed techniques that help to quell some of our situational anxiety, to shift from a "threat" mentality to an "opportunity" one. In Scare Your Soul, we offer a simple, actionable methodology of "positive reframing," where we shift a belief from a negative to a positive association through the use of vocabulary. Often, it's so simple that people discount its power.

Imagine someone approaching you as you are in the final preparations before speaking to a large group. You say instinctually, "Oh, I am so nervous!" That statement itself carries more weight than you might think. It reinforces your internal anxiety level. Now, given the same scenario, think of how you might react differently if you said, "You know, I'm nervous, but I'm also damn excited. I am the right person at the right time. Let's do this!"

When we utilize them at a time of anxiety, the words we use can help us experience our circumstances differently.

Tag-Removal Strategy: Reframe Anxiety as Excitement

Alison Wood Brooks, a professor of business administration in the negotiation, organizations, and markets unit at Harvard Business School, teaches a cutting-edge course in the school's MBA curriculum designed to help students hone four core conversational skills: topic selection, asking questions, levity, and kindness. As part of her ongoing research, Brooks studied how different types of self-talk affected performance before and after anxiety-producing activities like karaoke, answering complex math problems, and public speaking.

In one study, Brooks had subjects in her lab sing "Don't Stop Believin'"—Journey's 1981 classic—in front of an audience. Before they sang, a segment of the participants was asked to say out loud, "I'm really nervous about this." Another group of participants was prompted to say, "I'm really excited about this." A final subset stated, "I'm feeling really calm."[3] The study revealed that using the simple strategy of saying "I am excited" out loud generated more genuine enthusiasm for the daunting task. More importantly, they performed better, too.

The key? These distinct messages allow us to direct anxious energy into a mindset of "opportunity" rather than "threat."

Insight Exercise: Reframe a Procrastination

I invite you to think of a small action you have been putting off doing. Something that gives you the littlest tingles of anxiety when you think about it—when your whole internal world says, "I'm nervous. I can't do this." Once you've identified it, find a friend or accountability buddy and tell them about what you want to do. Tell them unequivocally and from the bottom of your soul, "I'm excited to do this." Get excited. Breathe in the excitement and breathe out the nerves.

How did that feel?

_____

_____

_____

_____

_____

Red Tag #3: "I Overthink Everything"

> In surrender, you no longer need ego defenses and false masks. You become very simple, very real. "That's dangerous," says the ego. "You'll get hurt. You'll become vulnerable." What the ego doesn't know, of course, is that only through the letting go of resistance, through becoming "vulnerable," can you discover your true and essential invulnerability. —ECKHART TOLLE

What are you thinking about *right now*?

I know you are engrossed in reading these words, but was your mind playing footsie with other thoughts or images, too? What's for dinner? Why has your toe been itching, why does your brother-in-law drive you crazy, which James Bond was really the best? (Sean Connery. No question.)

If you intentionally stop at any random point in your day and pay attention to your mind, you'll most likely experience one of 6,200 individual and distinct thoughts—psychologists have called them "thought worms"—that we conjure up every single day.

Not only are we obsessed with thinking, but researchers recently revealed that a whopping 47 percent of our thousands of thoughts are not even focused on things that are actually happening in our lives at the present moment! We are constantly role-playing, projecting, obsessing, worrying, fantasizing. It's no surprise that we refer to being "lost in thought."

These thought worms come into play often when we are obsessing about taking a scary action. Simply, overthinking stops us from positive action. In Buddhist discourse, this mental chattering is often termed the "monkey mind." It's the incessant, restless ego voice pounding inside our heads like a fifty-person drum circle outside a Phish concert.

Given free rein, our minds would keep it up, churning 24/7 in a never-ending cycle. If we quiet that voice, we'll avoid unhelpful, discursive decision-making and lean into rational and courageous decisions.

Tag-Removal Strategy: Find Your FRAME

In my experience of creating hundreds of courage challenges for Scare Your Soul, I've developed a thought exercise for slowing the racing of the mind, kindly calming our nervous system, and anchoring ourselves so we can make the right decisions.

The more you practice it, the more adept you will get.

You can remember this thought exercise with the concept called FRAME:

Find your anchor

Relax and refine

Accept your emotions

Motivate through an affirmation

Empty and act

Find Your Anchor

We immediately feel more grounded and secure when we encourage our parasympathetic nervous system to ratchet down. A few simple acts can "anchor" you in the moment, and you can begin to slow down.

- Sit in a chair or on a couch, with your feet placed flat on the ground.
- Place your hands on your knees, palms down.
- Smile—it helps.

Now, think about a time in your past when you were courageous. Really experience the moment. What was happening? How did it feel in your body?

Relax and Refine

Allow that memory to dissolve away. It's time to get centered and pay direct attention to the action you wish to take.

- Take several long breaths, feeling your lungs fill with air and then empty fully.
- Feel the air on your skin.
- Become aware of any small sounds around you.

Now, think about taking action. Visualize yourself being bold, brave, humble, and in service to yourself and your destiny. Watch yourself in your mind's eye. You can do this.

Accept Your Emotions

As we know from the work we have done so far, if we are growing, fear will always be our companion walking beside us. Accept kindly that this is the way.

- Your mind may feel on fire now, but we feel peace when we abide our fears.
- Every emotion you are feeling is right and true at this moment.

Allow emotions to flow through you, honoring them but allowing them to pass. They will.

Motivate through an Affirmation

Psychologists tell us that one of the greatest signifiers of habit change is our own belief that we have "agency." That we have the power within us to create real change. Now that you are calm and clear, focus on an affirmation that feels powerful to you:

- "I have the power to push past my barriers."
- "I am uniquely prepared to do this."
- "This is my time."
- "Each time I do this, my courage gets stronger."

Repeat the affirmation to yourself calmly and confidently. Keep doing so until you feel the certainty in your bones.

Empty and Act

Take another two deep breaths to calm yourself before the final step. Count to four on the inhalations and five on the exhalations.

Now you are ready to take the leap.

Insight Exercise: Put Your FRAME to the Test

Find one weekend day. Set four reminders on your phone for four different times during the day. When the reminder pings, immediately pay attention to what story or thought worm is in your mind at that moment. Write down exactly what you were thinking.

1. _____

2. _____

3. _____

4. _____

If any of the thoughts give you anxiety or feel overwhelming, practice the FRAME strategies: find your anchor, relax and refine, accept your emotions, motivate yourself through an affirmation, empty yourself, and then take an action that will lead to a positive reaction to your thoughts.

Write down your experience. What worked best? What was the hardest part?

_____

_____

_____

_____

_____

Red Tag #4: "I Am Going to Fail"

> What you think you create. What you feel you attract.
> What you imagine you become. —BUDDHA

Author and speaker Byron Katie has helped millions of people worldwide through a very simple process of self-inquiry. She calls this "The Work."[4]

Katie developed this practice at a time in her life when she was deeply depressed, burdened by a deep sense of dread and self-loathing. Waking one morning, she had a flash of insight: when she believed her thoughts, she suffered, and when she didn't, she was happy.

From this came four simple but powerful questions to ask about a belief that causes us pain.

1. *Is it true?*
2. *Can you absolutely know that it's true?*
3. *How do you react when you believe that thought?*
4. *Who would you be without the thought?*[5]

Tag-Removal Strategy: Interrogate Your Beliefs

The next time you bump up against a limiting or fear-based belief, stop and consider this: *In this moment, can I question and interrogate my thoughts? Can I separate them from me? Can I be courageous and actively challenge them?*

When you feel like you can answer yes, get a pen and paper and write down the limiting belief; keep it in front of you. Ask yourself Katie's four questions:

1. *Is it true?* Objectively, are you sure that what you wrote down is true?
2. *Can you absolutely know that it's true?* Really dig deep and be honest; is this belief an absolute certainty? What real evidence do you have to prove this belief is true?
3. *How do you react when you believe that thought?* This begins the real inquiry into cause and effect. What feelings come up when you believe this thought to be true? Anxiety, panic, fear?
4. *Who would you be without the thought?* How would your life be different if this thought weren't present? Would you feel freer, more confident, at peace?

Now ask yourself, *What do I prefer—life with or without this belief?*

Key Insights

1. The work of Scare Your Soul will create a sense of fear and anxiety; there is no doubt that these emotions will arise at some point. But we must press on and do the work.

2. Designing a courage avatar helps push past our anxious procrastinating. We all have sides to our personalities, and labeling and calling forth our courageous ones is an imaginative and useful way of moving to action.

3. When anxiety begins to take over and crowd out positive, courageous action, researchers find that reframing anxiety as excitement makes a difference. Simple hacks like speaking out loud to an accountability partner or breathing in a sense of excitement make a positive impact.

4. Using FRAME, you can calm the overthinking that plagues us and stops us from acting. We first find our anchors; then we relax and refine, visualizing ourselves taking the action. We intentionally accept all of our emotions in the moment, letting them flow before motivating ourselves with an affirmation. We can now breathe and take the leap.

5. When a long-held belief is causing you pain or pushing you to halt your courageous action, working through Byron Katie's simple four-question self-inquiry will help to illuminate whether your belief is rooted as solidly in fact as you thought. The questions open the possibility of actively choosing to analyze and remove it from your inner discourse. The outcome, regardless, is deeper, more honest self-awareness and empowerment.

CHAPTER 7

Screwing Up Is Sexy

> The most beautiful people we have known are those who have known defeat, known suffering, known struggle, known loss, and have found their way out of the depths. These persons have an appreciation, a sensitivity, and an understanding of life that fills them with compassion, gentleness, and a deep loving concern. Beautiful people do not just happen.
>
> ELISABETH KÜBLER-ROSS

I was back at the towering five-star hotel when I saw Derek again. I had been thinking about him. I'd also been thinking about his dream.

He was clad in his perfectly creased hotel uniform, walking down the long beige-and-cream lobby hallway studded with oversize black-and-white photographs of cityscapes. He bounded toward me, bypassing my outstretched hand, and gave me a hug.

"Thank you," he whispered in my ear. "I made the call."

It was just a month before that I stood in front of the hotel's entire staff—from the valet team and room service professionals to the top brass. I was there as a guest speaker, and it was my goal to encourage every one of them to push their boundaries. I wanted them to rightly believe that they could be the most empowered, most innovative, and yes, most courageous hotel staff in the country.

The hotel's restaurant served as our home base, and at the conclusion of the intense and powerful session together, I gave them a challenge: I asked pairs of professionals who held two very different types of roles to stand together in front of the room.

I encouraged them to commit publicly to one scary act in the following week that would unlock something special for them personally. Their "partner" would serve as their accountability buddy for that week. Together, the two would keep each other on track, and in doing so, build a relationship with one another. (This was an experience I had done many times with groups, but this day was special.)

One of the pairs included a top executive and a member of the room service staff. The executive voiced her commitment for the week. And then the server—Derek—told his story.

He loved his job at the hotel. It was a dream job in so many ways. But in his heart, he was an artist. He was a painter—a really good one, his mom would tell him—and his small apartment contained many canvases. It was something he never shared with co-workers until that afternoon.

I asked him, "So, what is your commitment? What is one thing that you are not doing because you are afraid?"

"Well, I have been thinking of calling an art gallery and seeing if there is any way that I could hang my paintings there sometime."

"And what is stopping you from picking up the phone?"

"Fear, I guess. That they will laugh. Or that they will just say no."

"So, fear of being rejected. Fear of failing in something that you want to happen. Here's the question: Is it worth the risk? The risk to be courageous and possibly fail? And if you made the commitment to do just that, and we supported you, is it something that you think you can do?"

After a brief pause, he said, "Yes. I can make the call."

A month later, we embraced in the hallway. He made that call, and the gallery had agreed. In fact, they *loved* his paintings.

· · ·

Nobody actually enjoys failing. Me included.

My personal list of failures is long and ignominious: I've developed projects that failed spectacularly. I've avoided commitment so strenuously that it ended loving relationships. I've turned down offers to do powerful work because it felt too risky. And I am a parent, which means I fail at something just about every day.

But the truth is, as much as my failures felt absolutely awful in the moment, each one in some way became the touchstone of my life. I've concluded:

- Failure has not made me less; I am more because of my flops.
- When I can actually celebrate my failures, my perfection pressure valve is released.
- Success feels easy; failure feels hard. But failure is the soil in which our greatest work grows.

An admission: If you take risks and push comfort zones, you will try things that end in failure. You will feel pain and discomfort. Expect it.

And that is the plan. I encourage you to screw up.

Why? Because screwing up means you're taking action.

You're admitting you don't have the answers, that you're taking the uncertain path, and that you are willing to embrace the magic of possibility. When you screw up, you can be bold, brave, and humble all at the same time.

Screwing up is, in a word, *sexy.*

In John C. Maxwell's book *Failing Forward*, he writes, "Determining what went wrong in a situation has value. But taking that analysis another step and figuring out how to use it to your benefit is the real difference maker when it comes to failing forward. Don't let your learning lead to knowledge; let your learning lead to action."[1]

Before we go any further, let's reflect on the nature of failure.

Writing Prompt: Confronting Failure

Describe a time when you confronted a fear of failure and still pushed through—when the risks seemed high, you couldn't possibly know the outcome, and yet you still acted.

_____

_____

_____

_____

_____

_____

_____

Embracing Our Inner Imposter

> I hope that in this year to come, you make mistakes....
>
> ...Make new mistakes. Make glorious, amazing mistakes. Make mistakes nobody's ever made before. Don't freeze, don't stop, don't worry that it isn't good enough, or it isn't perfect, whatever it is: art, or love, or work or family or life.
>
> Whatever it is you're scared of doing, Do it.
>
> —NEIL GAIMAN

From our first day as divorced co-parents, Laura and I really worked at being a united front.

We were open and honest, even when it was hard. We attended every school event together, talked daily about the kids, and crafted equitable schedules and holiday plans. When she remarried a terrific guy, Steve, I shared my enthusiasm and congratulations. They were both just as kind right back to me.

On my own, I worked hard, too. I met with a brilliant therapist, Suzanne, every week to make sure I was making good decisions. I plugged back into my spiritual community, read parenting books, created an environment at home where I hoped the kids would feel safe and loved.

The kids thrived. Laura and I were a team. And people seemed to notice.

I started to receive invitations from friends to meet for coffee. Then it was friends of friends. And then strangers. I learned quickly that "meet for coffee" was code for "My wife and I are getting divorced and I need to know what you did. You guys look like you're doing really well."

Five conversations led to seven, and then many more.

But all the time, although I thought that I was being helpful, I couldn't help but feel like a fraud. I would be in the middle of an animated conversation, and in the back of my mind, I was thinking, *Who am I to be some kind of divorce authority?*

When my dear friend Erica and I developed tandem women's and men's divorce support groups and began moderating larger group discussions, that nagging internal voice got louder. I kept pressing forward, earning a coaching certification. But even then, I could still hear the rumblings of the imposter.

I finally turned the corner when, in the middle of a conversation with a good friend who had confided in only me, I realized how blessed I was to be in these discussions at all. I began to slow down and stop focusing on problem solving. Instead, I would sit in rapt attention, witnessing other men courageously grappling with many of the same deep fears that I myself have confronted:

- What will happen if we divorce? What will my life be like?
- What if we stay together and I feel trapped forever?

- Am I screwing up my kids? Am I failing the ones I want to protect?
- What is life like being single? Is being unhappy better than being lonely?
- What happens if I lose all my friends?
- Will other people judge me?

Here I was, entering into what I can only call "holy conversations." I wasn't an imposter; I was making a difference.

An (Almost) Universal Experience

Imposter syndrome is the "belief that you are fraudulently claiming to be something that you are not, that you are not as good as other people think you are."[2] It is a belief that, no matter who you are or what your qualifications may be, you just don't belong. And given enough time, somebody is going to find out. And it is a secret shame that holds us back from leading a courageous life.

Imposter syndrome presents itself most in certain categories or groups. According to Valerie Young, author of *The Secret Thoughts of Successful Women: Why Capable People Suffer from the Impostor Syndrome and How to Thrive in Spite of It*,[3] the most susceptible and at-risk include:

- Under-represented groups (women, ethnic minorities, etc.)
- Students
- People with especially high-performing parents
- Academics
- People employed in creative fields
- People with unusually early career success
- First-generation college graduates and professionals
- Self-employed workers

And, although the above groups may have a higher propensity for "IS," I would argue that any of us who commit ourselves to courage-work will, at some point, feel like a fraud. We will, by the very nature of our bravery, be putting ourselves in places and situations which are new. We will feel uncomfortably unprepared.

Through many years of leading Scare Your Soul challenges, I've discovered a simple strategy to combat your inner imposter.

Stop thinking you're the only one who has an inner imposter.

You're in good company, my friend. You just have to see it. Almost everyone—including people who are in a place of growth in their lives—feels inadequate in some way. In fact, psychologists Pauline Rose Clance and Gail Matthews conducted research that found that seven in ten of us—from all walks of life—have felt like imposters for at least some part of our professional careers.[4]

Even people performing at the peak of their craft feel it:

- Starbucks CEO Howard Schultz said, "Very few people, whether you've been in that job before or not, get into the seat and believe today that they are now qualified to be the CEO. They're not going to tell you that, but it's true."[5]
- Maya Angelou said, "I have written eleven books, but each time I think, 'Uh-oh, they're going to find out now. I've run a game on everybody, and they're going to find me out.'"[6]
- Lady Gaga revealed, "I still sometimes feel like a loser kid in high school and I just have to pick myself up and tell myself that I'm a superstar every morning so that I can get through this day and be for my fans what they need for me to be."[7]
- Supreme Court justice Sonia Sotomayor admitted, "I have spent my years since Princeton, while at law school and in my various professional jobs, not feeling completely a part of the worlds I inhabit. I am always looking over my shoulder wondering if I measure up."[8]
- Tom Hanks said, "No matter what we've done, there comes a point where you think, 'How did I get here? When are they going to discover that I am, in fact, a fraud and take everything away from me?'"[9]

Celebrate how amazing you are.

Step into your power. Cop to the fact that you have skills and experiences that make you unique and well prepared to tackle the toughest life and career challenges. The key to defeating imposter syndrome is taking the time—and having the guts—to recognize how you shine. You'll practice this in our next challenge—taking time to "brag" about yourself.

Scare Your Soul Challenge: Creating Your Brag Sheet

This is your time to declare how amazing you are. We're taught to be humble. I know it's not easy to brag about yourself. But do it! Prolific self-help author Danielle LaPorte calls this "Glory Boarding" and offers the opportunity to brag about victories and accomplishments.[10] Let's do it!

In the past year, I…

Learned:

_____

_____

Created:

_____

_____

Inspired:

_____

_____

Won:

_____

_____

Transformed:

_____

_____

Gave:

_____

_____

Studied:

_____

_____

Saw:

_____

_____

Wrote:

_____

_____

Found:

_____

_____

Led:

_____

_____

Opened:

_____

_____

Closed:

_____

_____

Shared:

_____

Healed:

_____

_____

Connected:

_____

_____

Taught:

_____

_____

Built:

_____

_____

Wowed:

_____

_____

Developed:

_____

_____

Add anything else that applies:

_____

_____

_____

_____

Dahlia Quits and Finds Courage

I had the kind of job some people dream about. Once, I spoke at an annual conference, and an intimate cohort of three next-generation young women leaders specializing in the same field followed me from the podium into the restroom, asking questions about my work and telling me they wished to be just like me when they grew up.

But the truth was I didn't even want to be like me.

Every day I dressed up in a black suit and sensible heels—a costume for my charade—to play the part of someone with an apparently enviable life. I was living an idea of what success looked like, but not my idea. So I quit. (Insert cricket noises here.) Rumor had it I was fired. That's how crazy scary it was to quit my job.... People in my community assumed I was fired because no one in their right mind would actually quit.

Fear had guided me for my entire life, and I ended up trapped inside one I didn't want. Courage freed me; it gave me language around what I was feeling and welcomed me into a community of people who admired stepping outside of comfort zones to push myself into the life I deserved.

It doesn't matter if I am now a professional chef, snake charmer, or wrestler—or all of those things. Because the only person I must impress is me.

Living courageously is about pushing yourself to discover the life you deserve to live—as fully and openly and honestly as any human being can. To Scare Your Soul is to find yourself within yourself by pushing beyond the ideas that hold you captive.

Living courageously is permission to be authentic and free.

Finding Purpose in Failure

I am not concerned that you have fallen. I am concerned that you arise. —ABRAHAM LINCOLN

Scare Your Soul is, in many ways, about giving up ease in exchange for the hard-fought.

Like passing up a five-lane expressway in favor of a long, winding back road with no GPS service, the choices that we make—and why we make them—determine both how we show up in our lives and where life takes us.

Fear of failure, while very real to us as it arises in our bodies and minds, is born from attachment to a prescribed outcome.

It is universal; it's part of being human, and it can be overcome. Try this: when you start to feel the familiar tug of the fear of failure begin to take hold, altering your sense of self and your decision-making process, sit with it. Now let's go deeper. Give these strategies a try:

Give yourself a break: Understand your innate desire to succeed, to perform at your best, to accomplish your goals. Know that you can only do your best in any given circumstance.

Detach from the outcome: Focus on the emotions that arise, honor them, let them wash over your body and spirit. And then, unleash yourself from your desired outcome. Can you feel a loosening, a sense of ease, when you open yourself to the concept of "whatever happens is OK"?

Dig below the surface: Ask yourself, *Why am I* really *feeling this fear? What drives the fear? Is it…*

- Fear of taking the action.
- Fear of disappointing others.
- Fear of loss of social status.
- Fear of being talked about by others.
- Fear of losing financial status or a job?

Find the lesson: No matter what the outcome of any of our travails, there is a lesson to be learned. You can find it. It just takes time and some reflection. Ask yourself: What do I know now that I didn't know before? And how I am stronger and wiser from having this experience? Soon enough, it will come.

Key Insights

1. In a life that is dedicated to pushing comfort zones, failure is inevitable. But letting the fear of failure stop you isn't.

2. We are biologically predisposed to avoid failure. But through practiced interventions, we can combat our physical responses to the fear of failure, radically changing how we live with failure, and even embrace it.

3. A key component that drives our fear of failure is our imposter syndrome. We can overcome this insidious force by understanding that everyone—even high performers in every field—feels it, and by getting grounded in our own impressive qualities and accomplishments.

4. Finding fun in the midst of the fear of failure turns negative emotions into positive ones.

5. One of the most powerful positive forces in the human mindset is one of purpose. When we feel that an activity has meaning—for ourselves or others—we push through fear more courageously. Seeing failure as a necessary step in growth, and the lessons that it provides as critical to our forward momentum, radically alters the paradigm.

PART III

Taking Action

Seven Principles for Leading a Scare Your Soul Life

CHAPTER 8

Courage Principle One: Gratitude

This is a wonderful day. I've never seen this one before.

—MAYA ANGELOU

When the email landed in my inbox, I had to read it twice. It was so unexpected that I glanced around me, fearing that I was getting punked. Little did I know that it would signal the change of how I would spend every night of my life from that point forward.

"Scott," the email read, "my name is Carly. You don't know me, but I really need to meet you. Please say yes. How about I meet you at your house this Saturday night at 10:00?"

Now, in my younger days, I might have been less skeptical. I probably would have been jazzed about some romantic possibility or been swayed by my hyperactive sense of curiosity. But deep into my forties and hopefully just a bit wiser, I knew that some minor due diligence was necessary. So, I did what any reasonable person would do: I pulled up Facebook to see if "Carly" actually existed.

As it turns out, she certainly did. Carly—as best I could tell through my scan of her profile photos—was a happily married mom of three. In her photos, she seemed blissful, always smiling. Although I was sure we had never met, we did share a number of Facebook friends. So I picked up the phone and called one of them.

"Ethan," I asked, "tell me about Carly."

"Well, I don't know her that well," he told me, "but she seems really cool. Funky, with lots of tattoos. She has three kids. I heard that one of them is really sick."

It was that last statement that really caught my attention. I thanked Ethan and sat to think for a minute. So many times in my early life, I closed down every opportunity that felt odd or uncomfortable. Even if it meant helping someone. *Not anymore.*

I picked up my phone again, and pecked out a message back. "Sure, Carly. Happy to meet you. 10:00 PM Saturday night. My house. See you then."

I could barely wait until the weekend. I ran through scenarios in my mind: *What could this be about? Was she thinking of romance? Did she have some secret? Is it something about her child? Did she have some terrible news about me or my family and need to tell me in person?*

Finally, after an interminably long wait, Saturday night arrived. At 10:00 p.m. on the dot, I heard her knock. My French bulldog, Morty, padded along next to me as I walked nervously through my kitchen and to the front door.

As I opened, I saw Carly's absolutely beguiling smile. She had blond hair that cascaded past her shoulders, and wore ripped jeans and a white T-shirt. Tattoos trailed down her arms.

"I'm Carly," she said simply and directly. "We need to talk."

She seemed so confident, so sure of herself and her intentions, that despite how insanely awkward this whole scene was playing out, I opened the door wide. She stepped inside.

I led her back through my kitchen. I debated where to sit. *Formally on chairs? No, just be cool.* I pointed to my uncomfortably small living room couch. She kicked off her Birkenstocks and we sat facing each other. For the first time, in the light, I noticed her eyes. Open, inquisitive, inviting. Just then, Morty jumped up on the couch between us and began ferociously licking her feet. She laughed out loud. He licked harder.

As this barefooted stranger squealed with delight on my tiny living room couch, I had to laugh myself. *What the hell would this night bring?*

After I was able to extricate Morty's tongue from between Carly's toes, she told me why she needed to meet with such urgency. "It is a soul mission," she said. "I was told to call you. By the universe."

Now, I have experienced my share of new-age dialogue in my many yoga retreats and meditation workshops, but this had me confused. I needed to know more.

From that moment on, sitting on that couch—what she would later call a "magic couch"—we talked for three straight hours.

Carly was deep, kind, and outrageously funny. She was open and vulnerable.

She also told me why it was so important to her to meet with me. She told me that she had seen some of the experiences with Scare Your Soul that I had posted on Facebook, and felt like I was someone who could really listen to her. Someone who maybe could help her find the courage she needed in her life.

She was unhappy, she revealed. Devastatingly unhappy. Her marriage was on the brink of collapse, and she was worried about the prospect of divorce and what it would mean to her children... and to her. She was sad and scared. She needed hope. And courage.

I told her about the concept of the "blank page," about our unique ability to move through transitions, not as ending points, but as beautifully fresh new chapters that we alone can write. I told her that, despite the pain and chaos a divorce might foster, her three sons could be a "North Star" for Carly and her co-parent. That most of us tend to sail into the unpredictable waters of bitterness and resentment after our divorces, but our children's best interests can become the North Star that keeps both parents focused on what really matters.

And her openness and vulnerability invited my own right back.

I shared how so often I felt like a complete failure as a dad. How some days were so busy and my organizational and planning skills were so poor I could only muster dinosaur-shaped chicken nuggets dipped in ketchup for their dinner. An ideal dad would be taking time to talk to and teach his children, so why was I so consistently putting them in front of a Scooby-Doo video so that I could just get the laundry done?

I shared how getting divorced initially made me feel like I would never find someone to love again. How I felt like damaged goods, how I would have to admit for the rest of my life that I couldn't make my marriage work, and that divorce brought back those wretched feelings of inadequacy from my youth.

At 1:00 a.m., we smiled. We stood and stretched for a moment, and walked stiffly together to the front door.

As Carly stepped from the warm light of my house to the darkness of the front porch, she said one of the most meaningful things I had ever heard.

"Tonight I found my soul-brother."

And then, as almost an afterthought, she said, "Listen, this upcoming week is going to be hell. I need something to look forward to. I loved what you said about a gratitude practice. How about I send you five things I am grateful for each night for a week, and you do the same?"

"Sure. Why don't we just text them to each other? You'll get through the week. I promise."

The next night, I sent her the following:

I am grateful for…

1. The people who are "smilers"—like Vicki K, who smiles EVERY time I see her in the hallway at the kids' school.
2. The feeling that I am almost dancing—my sweat flying everywhere—when I am pummeling my boxing coach's mitts.
3. The sensation of warm, humid air hitting my skin in the morning when I walk Morty.

4. The moments of supreme peace I feel just after I put my kids to bed, tiptoeing quietly down the dark hallway so as not to wake them.

5. Doing all the hard things. Not always succeeding. But always trying.

Carly sent me hers. We continued for a few days. We shared more.

I found that I really liked spending time each day thinking about what I would write that night. Amidst the petty frustrations and mindless tasks my life generated, I was slowing down. I was paying attention to the things that would typically fly under my own personal radar. I was developing my ability to notice those really delicious moments of my life.

In my gratitude texts, I was fully open. So was Carly. Our lists were peppered with gratitudes about passions, dreams, sex, moments of meaning, parenting joys and challenges, the acceptance of our own insecurities, unexpected triumphs, small moments of beauty or connection. Our gratitudes gave both of us permission to be fully ourselves; this was not a social media post but a true partnership, where our spiritual contract was based on total honesty about what was unfolding in our lives.

I found myself actually contacting the people I would write about in my gratitudes. I did reach out to Vicki K and tell her, "I just want to let you know I love how much you smile." Inevitably, that interaction would end up in a warm hug.

It felt like ripples of goodness.

After our one week of gratitude grew to a close, Carly sent me this text: "Should we do it for another week?"

"Absolutely."

We did do it for another week. And then another.

And, yes, I have, at times, dropped off my responsibilities because life somehow got in the way. Carly would call me out: "Did your fingers break?"

With that, I would be back on track.

At the time of this writing, we have been texting five gratitudes every night for *seven years*. Seven years of nightly practice—living and then cataloguing thirteen thousand individual gratitudes—has changed me forever.

As we explore what gratitude is, I want you to know very clearly what gratitude is not. It is not a rationale to stay in an abusive or toxic relationship, an unfulfilling job, an unsafe home environment. Gratitude is the appreciation for what is good, healthy, and positive in life, and it should reinforce those elements. Furthermore, gratitude should never be a lever for others in our lives to stifle our growth because they believe we should "just be happy with the way things are." Gratitude is active, growth-enhancing, and transformational. It is a positive power that exists within every individual.

How Gratitude Scares Our Soul

Gratitude is the understanding that many millions of things come together and live together and mesh together and breathe together in order for us to take even one more breath of air. —DAVID WHYTE

If I said the word *gratitude* to you, what would come to mind? Not too long ago, I posed this question to our Scare Your Soul community and received many different responses:

"Being able to really say thank you and mean it."
"Being appreciative for what we have."
"Not taking things for granted."

"Thanking God for the blessings I have in my life."
"Knowing that others have helped me, and recognizing that."

These are all absolutely true. But my goal in this chapter is to inspire you to see gratitude as a daily, courageous act. To toss it on its ear. To see its boldness and its ability to transform the way you see and lead your life, such that you might answer the question this way:

"Practicing gratitude can be hard, sticky, and scary."
"Gratitude teaches me to let go of my sense of control."
"Gratitude allows me to see things as they really are."
"Gratitude thrusts new ideas into my consciousness."
"Gratitude has transformed me into more of the person I am, not the person others want me to be."

The impact of gratitude is experienced every day by people around the world. Just think of the foundations of so many of our major world religions; most are rooted in the feeling and expression of gratitude. Central to Christian practices is the Eucharist ("thanksgiving" in Greek); followers of Islam participate in Ramadan, the monthlong celebration of thanks; the first Jewish prayer spoken in the morning is the *Modeh Ani* ("I give thanks"); there is a sense of deep gratitude cultivated through Buddhist mindfulness practices; from a natural perspective, John Muir shared his transcendent natural experiences amidst the redwoods.

Each one of us has the innate capacity to feel grateful, if for no other reason than the fact that everything we have done, learned, and accomplished in life was due to the good graces (or at least the good intentions) of someone else. Someone else helped us learn to eat, speak, walk, and run. Someone else grew the wheat for our bread, sewed our clothing, invented the Internet, designed the tracks under our subway car, and baked the delicious chocolate brownies on the table in the break room.

Gratitude is also one of the most well-researched emotions in psychology's modern era. Robert Emmons, psychology professor at the University of California, Davis, and the man who has probably conducted more gratitude research than anyone else alive, explains that there are two key components of practicing gratitude:[1]

1. Affirming the good things we've received in our lives
2. Acknowledging the role other people play in providing our lives with goodness

The very act of focusing on gratitude is transformational. By acknowledging in specific and consistent ways how people provide for us, we begin to gain a deeper appreciation for everything around us.

Gratitude changes us.

It opens our senses to the world around us like a key. It taps into the foundation of our ancestors' traditions and identity.

And almost more than anything else, gratitude *wakes us up*.

Waking Up

> You pray in your distress and in your need; would that you
> might pray also in the fullness of your joy and in your days
> of abundance. —KAHLIL GIBRAN

We've lived through crisis before, you and me.

Maybe we were leading our everyday lives, and unbidden, someone we cared about deeply suddenly passed away. Maybe we lost a job. Maybe we received a call from our doctor with an unwanted diagnosis. And for those of us who experienced a global pandemic, we have all lived through a time of crisis together.

In such moments, we come face-to-face with the reality that something has changed and may never return. We ask ourselves questions like these:

Why didn't I say "I love you" more?

Why didn't I spend more time?

Why didn't I walk into that job I loved so much with a smile
more often?

Why didn't I treasure the small things before they got taken away?

That very moment is when we awaken. A sense of gratitude washes over us like a great wave, and for a time—a moment, a day, a week—we see with clear eyes what is really important. Winston Churchill said, "Never let a good crisis go to waste." And right he was.

But dear reader, who wants to sit idly by like Vladimir and Estragon in Beckett's *Waiting for Godot*, waiting for a crisis to wake us up when we have the alarm right by our bedside?

Writing Prompt: Think of a Time When You Didn't Let "a Good Crisis" Go to Waste

I invite you to delve back into a time when it took a crisis to make you feel grateful, when something had to shock you into realizing the value of something so important in your life.

_____

_____

_____

_____

_____

_____

_____

The Practice

You're sitting in your doctor's office waiting for your appointment, and as always, they are late.

It seemed to take years off your life to fight through traffic just to get here on time, and it's already been fifteen minutes. The waiting room is sterile, lifeless. There are those same magazines from your last appointment, read and haphazardly tossed on the coffee table: *Better Homes and Gardens, Reader's Digest, People.* You look at your watch. It's two minutes later than the last time you checked. And there's no Wi-Fi.

As you look up, you notice something. A small flower had been placed in a tiny vase and is sitting on the window ledge. Just one flower…a daisy, you think. White, with a brilliant yellow center.

Maybe you think, *That's odd. Random, yes. But nice.*

You have a choice in this moment. You can dive back into your routine mental gymnastics about how frustrated you are. Or you can stop, pay attention, and feel grateful.

How can a single flower on a doctor's office window ledge invite gratitude? Stop and ask yourself these questions:

- Think back. How did it feel when you placed a single flower into the hand of someone you loved, or nervously pinned a corsage or boutonniere on your prom date's dress or lapel under the watchful eye of your date's parents? Can you inhabit that place in time?
- How about this: Did you ever hike up a steep, rocky hill only to find a patch of flowers growing through the boulders?
- Were you ever sick in the hospital, sequestered in a room alone, only to receive a bouquet of flowers from the gift shop, reminding you that someone cared?
- Did you know that there are over four hundred thousand different varieties of flowers on earth at this very moment, and one of them—the pale violet *Silene tomentosa*—was thought to be extinct, but was found again 1994 in a small preserve

in Gibraltar? Or that its seed is saved at the Millennium Seed Bank in Kew, England, and is being grown back into existence near the place it was re-found?

Writing Prompt: Practicing Gratitude

List five things you are grateful for in your life at this very moment.

1. _____

2. _____

3. _____

4. _____

5. _____

Choose one and write for yourself why you are so grateful.

_____

_____

_____

_____

_____

The Steps

> Gratitude is a sort of laughter of the heart. —DAVID BROOKS

From my experience, the practice of gratitude isn't an amorphous process. It is actually a manageable set of steps:

1. **Being actively aware:** We must be awake and aware in our own lives to identify the goodness around us. So many of us sleepwalk through our existence, bound to routine, using our

mental awareness to overthink and ruminate rather than to pay attention. Take time; slow down. Give yourself space to see what is around you, the interactions with others and what they mean in the moment, the nontangible gifts that nature, spirituality, and community give to you. Take a breath, pay attention, and just be aware.

2. **Feeling the feeling:** After we identify something that brings goodness into our lives, the next step is to pay attention again. But this time, it is to the feeling that swells within us when we recognize it. How do you feel in the moment? And where in your body or heart does that feeling sustain itself? Where does it feel the strongest and most potent? This is true body-mind awareness.

3. **Savoring:** Think of savoring an experience as you might think of taking a bite of your favorite dessert. Mine, to be completely candid, is coconut cream pie. When I think of taking a forkful of it, I can almost taste the dense, buttery graham cracker crust, the cool tang of the golden-hued custard, the four-inch layer of fresh whipped cream burnished gold on its top with shavings of toasted coconut. That feeling I am having right now? Savoring. Really slowing down and enjoying each moment.

4. **Thanking:** Most gratitude practices fail to include this final step, but it is one of the most important. Reaching out and thanking from our hearts creates ripples throughout the world. When we thank someone for bringing goodness into our world—from the parent who birthed us to the employee at the physician's office who decided to place a flower on the window ledge—we create a ripple effect. We thank someone, they feel valued and meaningful, they then reach out to someone in their life who, in turn, feels valued and meaningful… and on and on. As mathematician and meteorologist Edward

Lorenz theorized about the "butterfly effect," one small action can potentially reverberate and create change throughout the world.[2]

Writing Prompt: Gratitude Illuminators

In a journal, take some time to reflect on and answer the following questions, which will shed some light on your experience with gratitude:

1. Most of us spend our weeks looking forward to the weekend. Write about ten things that are great about Monday mornings.
2. Imagine that there is a brand-new technology just invented that allows us to feel grateful just by pushing a button on our phones. How would you use it? How often? How would your life be different from what it is now?
3. Finish this sentence: "It's an amazing day when I..."
4. What is one thing that you're really grateful someone taught you that you can now teach or pass on to someone else?

Scare Your Soul Challenge: Find a Gratitude Partner

It takes courage to have a gratitude partner.

If you practice real, true, authentic, vulnerable gratitude, it shines a light deep into your soul. By choosing my nightly practice with Carly, I am showing both her and me what is important to me, what lights me up, what challenges are turning into opportunities. I share it all unabashedly. And in doing so, I've had some revelations:

When I practice authentic gratitude, I am happier and more present. I still have days full of frustration, and yes, I still can take things for granted, but on the whole, I find myself appreciating life more.

Gratitude flips your conceptions. It asks you to find some amount of value in people and experiences that you didn't like, agree with, or want as a part of your life. How hard is it for you to feel gratitude toward your relatives with polar opposite political views? Gratitude leads us to a place of more compassion and understanding.

Gratitudes don't always have to be positive. Feeling grateful for acknowledging and surviving a challenging time is immensely powerful. In fact, as Carly and I have progressed, more than half of our gratitudes are about the challenges that we face; we know now that they, indeed, will be the times that will teach us, fuel us, and make us more empathetic humans.

You have to choose it. As we discussed previously, there are important steps in fully experiencing gratitude, and they are not always evident in the rush of our busy days. Not practicing gratitude is like having a Ferrari (feel free to substitute your own dream car here) fully gassed in your garage but never actually taking it for a spin.

So, I would invite you to be bold and ask someone to be your gratitude partner for a week. When they agree, commit to sending each other five gratitudes each night by whatever means you like (I happen to like texts, but you may prefer email, instant messages, or even calling each other and sharing verbally). Your goal is to do this every night for seven days. Do not repeat your gratitudes; rather, choose five new ones every night.

Lean into truth and vulnerability.

Dave Reaches Deep for Gratitude

It was 5:00 p.m. on April 30, 2020, at the height of the pandemic's first wave. The country was in lockdown. I was pacing the kids' playroom, pretending to be present with my son building Magna-Tiles but waiting for my phone to ring.

I felt the buzzing in my pocket and saw "Papago Pediatrics." I ran outside as the doctor said, "Hi, is this Cooper's dad?"

I nervously sat down. My wife followed me out the door. We were hoping, praying...for good news.

Our daughter had awakened a week prior with a limp. We figured she hurt her leg playing with her brother, running around outside, doing what little kids do. The pediatrician said it was nothing to worry about, but if it persisted for over a week, be sure to get blood work. Well, it persisted.

The doctor said, "We looked at your daughter's blood work and the results are very worrisome."

My wife heard the doctor's words and she started crying. Through her tears, she asked in a whisper, "Is it leukemia?"

"I think so," the doctor replied.

To hear your three-year-old daughter has cancer: How is that possible? How is that fair? How was this happening?

So began our journey into one of a parent's worst fears. But I can tell you we found the courage to survive, and this is the advice that changed everything for us.

On day one after the diagnosis, another parent who had successfully walked a child through cancer treatment told us, "If you need to cry, go in another room. Young children don't respond to fear and sadness. They respond to love and joy and positivity."

This would be the bravest act of our lives.

To recognize every time we felt fear and consciously choose love. I've been in the wellness world for twenty years. I've written books about this stuff. But this was different. This was life-threatening.

Through all the challenges of my daughter losing her hair, getting nauseous as hell from the chemo, spending weeks at a time in a tiny hospital room during the height of the pandemic isolated from everyone...again and again, we learned and practiced making the choice. It didn't always come easy.

But we could feel our daughter's heart opening.

She was softer and kinder and more loving during her treatment than she ever was before it. She told us after visiting with a boy also going through cancer treatment, "I feel love in my heart." Whatever we needed to do to nurture that feeling, we were all in.

It sounds so obvious, but there were ways we used to let the busyness and distractions and arguments get between us and our children.

I'm a forty-eight-year-old father of young children. I'm always tired but constantly reminded every time I see my daughter's newly grown and flowing blond hair that parenthood is a blessing and an honor, not a burden.

We resolve conflicts more quickly because while arguing is part of everyday family dynamics, it is not conducive to healing. We do our best to have meals together, to slow down at bedtime, to call each other out when we let the little things take up our bandwidth.

Fast-forward to the present moment. Cooper is in remission. She is in school, having playdates, playing soccer, and living her best and healthiest life.

During the scariest time in our lives, we are so grateful for modern medicine. But even better is modern medicine supported by love. And we know now more than ever, that is the best treatment in the world.

Ongoing Gratitude Practice(s)

Let gratitude be the pillow upon which you kneel to say your nightly prayer. —MAYA ANGELOU

The last challenge in this chapter calls on you to view gratitude as a long-term engagement.

Gratitude, as we know, is a lifelong pursuit; therefore, I am putting my cards on the table: Here are twenty-five gratitude experiences. As you continue through this book—and through your life after the book is done—step back into this chapter. Choose one practice to do when you feel the need for a boost of positivity and gratitude in your life...and check off that you've done it.

When you are done with all of them, email me at scott@scare yoursoul.com and let me know about your experience.

That being said, you will be the recipient of the goodness that will arise.

1. Think of one person who was a mentor to you. Call them and thank them. Be specific in the ways they helped. Make them feel great for their efforts.
2. Respond to an email from ten years ago. Tell the sender you were thinking about them.
3. Write a Post-it Note sharing one thing you are grateful for and place it on every family member's pillow.
4. Reflect on this quote from Toni Morrison's novel *Tar Baby*: "At some point in life the world's beauty becomes enough. You don't need to photograph, paint, or even remember it. It is enough." Then, spend 10 minutes outside drinking in that quote.
5. Remove all the friends from your social media who don't contribute to your feeling of gratitude, and send messages to ten who do.
6. Do one random act of kindness. Don't tell anyone about it. Reflect on it and feel grateful for your own efforts.
7. Cancel a scheduled appointment and instead spend the time with someone you love. Tell them how grateful you are for them.
8. Spend one hour less indulging in mindless viewing or scrolling, and one hour more in a gratitude meditation (you can find many of them for free on YouTube).

9. Share your gratitude journey with someone else. Inspire them.

10. Buy a postcard, write a kind message, and send it to someone you love.

11. Set the alarm on your phone for a random time. When it goes off, think a grateful thought.

12. Commit to one day when you won't complain…or gossip.

13. Try to read a newspaper online in another language. Smile if you understand something. Feel grateful that you are fluent in at least one language, and what language does for you.

14. Drop a dozen donuts off with someone you haven't seen in a while.

15. Wash dishes mindfully, loving the warm water and lots of bubbles. Be happy and indulge it as if it were a favorite experience.

16. Volunteer at a homeless shelter. As you do, reflect on how truly lucky you are.

17. Buy a coffee for the person behind you in a coffee shop. And tell the barista how thankful you are that they are so good at what they do.

18. Talk with a veteran about their experiences. Really listen.

19. Buy some of the candies of your childhood. Enjoy the moment and the memories.

20. Donate to one good cause this month just because you were asked. Feel generous when you do.

21. Give someone at work the spotlight. Really show they are valued.

22. Help a friend understand how important they are.

23. Find a nice handwritten letter that someone sent you; send it back to them with a beautiful note of your own.

24. Instead of saying just "thank you" today, say, "I want to tell you how much I appreciate you."

25. Cook someone's favorite meal and invite them to dinner. Share stories of meals that you were really grateful for.

Key Insights

1. Gratitude is one of the most powerful, most well-researched of human emotions. Rooted in the concept of thankfulness, it has two main components: affirming the good things we've received in our lives and acknowledging the role other people play in providing our lives with goodness.

2. Experiences of gratitude can be triggered in a number of ways, including how we react to moments of crisis or high emotion.

3. The process of fully embracing gratitude has several steps, which follow in a sequential order: actively noticing, feeling the feelings, savoring those feelings deeply, and then thanking those who are responsible for the goodness we have received.

4. A gratitude practice involving a partner can be a life-changing experience. Focusing on small, repeated expressions of thankfulness—as specific as possible—seals in the daily benefits.

CHAPTER 9

Courage Principle Two: Adventure

Live your life by a compass, not a clock.

—STEPHEN COVEY

Tommy Rivers Puzey walked toward the starting line of the New York City Marathon in November 2021. For the elite ultrarunner with dozens of wins already in the can, one would think this would be just another in a long line of 26.2-mile jaunts. It certainly wasn't. A little more than one year before, he was diagnosed with an aggressive form of lymphoma that would threaten his life.[1]

The former marathon champion many times over endured chemotherapy, was put into a medically induced coma, and spent grueling weeks in rehab, relearning nearly every body movement as if he were an infant. Along the way, he had time to think. To ponder the beauty and majesty of being alive. Of being able to even take a breath. Of the multitude of people and experiences that bring us love. So, in November, just fifteen months from his life-altering diagnosis, he approached the starting line. In what was the most challenging race he would ever tackle, he was determined to finish, and in the cold and dark of Central Park, he did.

He would tell the *New York Times* that the race wasn't about mile markers but about "moving from dot to dot to dot between these expressions of love and inspiration."[2]

Theologian Martin Buber once wrote, "All journeys have secret destinations of which the traveler is unaware."[3] And if we think about it, isn't that what we want in life? To enjoy, to thrill in "moving from dot to dot," living our days with wonder, excitement, and zest? To live in the present moment as much as we possibly can, drinking in all that it offers to us?

I invite you to lead your life with a sense of adventure. I encourage you to embrace the open seas, the wrong turns, the unexpected vistas.

Consider asking yourself the following:

What will happen if I get lost instead of always having to know where I'm going?
What if I followed my heart and my excitement instead of my planned route?
What can I give up or put down to lighten my load?
Who will I meet, what will I experience, what shall I taste?
How can I find adventure in my own life, in my own mind?

There are ways to courageously see our lives as adventures (you've already done it, as you will see), to embrace the unexpected ninety-degree turns, to revere the sense of uncertainty inherent in adventure.

In a 2021 podcast with Rich Roll, Tommy Rivers Puzey said, "Our capacity to be happy is to recognize life as it is happening."[4]

Let's begin that work by first looking back and honoring what we have indeed already accomplished.

The Road Map of Your Life

Life is not measured by the number of breaths we take, but by the moments that take our breath away. —MAYA ANGELOU

Radha Agrawal is the co-founder, CEO, and chief community architect of Daybreaker. I first heard about her when I attended a Daybreaker event, which are drug- and alcohol-free, early-morning raves held in cities around the world. They attract stressed-out, adventurous people into vacant warehouses and empty bars for dancing and connecting before their day jobs commence. She has built a tremendous global community around her healthy concept. In her book, *Belong*, she introduces the concept of a "life timeline," a visual map of our lives beginning with our births and progressing through our childhoods, relationships, careers, and key milestones.[5]

In creating our own life timelines, we get to see a bird's-eye view of where we have been and what we have accomplished.

Scare Your Soul Challenge: Create Your Own Life Timeline

Radha's version focuses on more traditional milestones (first job, first home, first marriage), but I'd like us to expand our lens. For example, I want you to consider adding things like these:

- The first time you remember speaking up in school
- A travel experience that was meaningful, edifying, or exciting
- Gaining autonomy for the first time
- Saying I love you for the first time
- Doing something that terrified you
- Career or other changes that pushed your comfort zone
- An epic failure
- 9/11, the Covid pandemic, or other world events that scared you
- A bad breakup or the beginning of a deep friendship
- Doing something crazy that you'll never forget
- Death or loss of important people in your life
- Births of your children and/or grandchildren
- Empty nesting, retiring, or changing your path completely

Choose ten milestones in the upcoming spaces, or—if you're so bold—open your journal and write one milestone for every year you've been alive.

In the beginning, I was born!

Year/Milestone: _____

Year/Milestone: _____

Year/Milestone: _____

Year/Milestone: _____

Year/Milestone: _____

Year/Milestone: _____

Year/Milestone: _____

Year/Milestone: _____

Year/Milestone: _____

Year/Milestone: _____

What was the most surprising milestone that made it to your road map? Why?

_____

_____

What milestone felt like the biggest failure when it happened?

_____

_____

Where on your road map did you feel the biggest surge of confidence?

_____

_____

What was the saddest milestone? Why?

_____

_____

Looking at your road map as a whole, how do you feel?

_____

_____

Finding Adventure in Our Daily Lives

> I may not have gone where I intended to go, but I think I
> have ended up where I intended to be. —DOUGLAS ADAMS

The biggest myth about leading an adventurous life is that we must travel to experience one. The truth is, adventure is a state of mind, not a set of driving directions, and we can begin in small but powerful ways.

To see what I mean, in the next day, try these on for size:

- To prepare, find a photo of one moment of adventure you've had, and tape it to your mirror.
- Begin the day by waking up early. Drink in the quietness.
- Vary as many of your most basic routines as you can (brush your teeth with your nondominant hand, take a completely different route to work).
- Put on an outfit or a hat that shows your true personality, even if you think it's completely crazy.
- Remove your cell phone from the mix; place it on vibrate and only use it when you absolutely have to.

When you are done with the day, take a few moments to reflect. You didn't take a trip to Bali or Berlin.... You just lived your life.

But you did it with an eye toward adventure!

Adventuring Inside

The first half of life is devoted to forming a healthy ego, the second half is going inward and letting go of it.

—CARL JUNG

It was getting late on New Year's Eve, and I was ready to bolt.

My typical New Year's Eve celebrations were far from calm affairs. One was spent snaking my way through New Orleans from Bourbon Street to Jackson Square amidst throngs of others; another was carousing with revelers in London's Trafalgar Square; still another was spent wiping tear gas from my eyes after getting caught up in an unexpected riot in Athens, Greece.

But here I was in New York City, sitting cross-legged on a yoga mat at the Jivamukti Yoga School near Union Square. I leaned over to peer out of the second-floor window. Below, I could see streets teeming with people. I brought my gaze back to my mat and then to the wide and long hall. I was surrounded by people ready for a very different type of New Year's experience.

Each year on the holiday, the center hosted a special evening of meditation to release the year past and prepare for the new year ahead. Having been in the city for several days for work, I decided this *inner* adventure might be an interesting way to spend an evening usually scheduled for champagne and revelry.

But as I settled onto my mat surrounded by strangers, each of us descending into our own solitary bubble of silence, I just wanted to leave. The silent meditation, they announced, would be three and a half hours long. It would be unguided. Just sitting. My work friends were all out on the town, and here I was, alone on a yoga mat. The doors closed and the lights dimmed right as I was about to make a run for it.

It was 8:30 p.m., and the massive hall was lit only by the tiny white lights that ran the length of the walls. Stuck now, I settled in. The room—even though it was packed with well over a hundred people—was pristinely quiet.

With nothing to do but sit in silence, over the next three and a half hours, I went on an adventure.

In my mind, I relived my childhood, I experienced vibrant memories of my grandparents, I rediscovered long-forgotten awkward teen moments, the birth of my children, amazing moments with good friends.

At midnight, a bell rang. I opened my eyes. I smiled. Actually, I couldn't stop smiling.

As I walked through Union Square back to my hotel, I couldn't help but thank myself for the gift of the time and space to go on this adventure—one that didn't require going anywhere.

Now it's your turn:

Insight Exercise: What Does Your Inner Adventure Look Like?

1. Find a comfortable position, whether it be lying down, sitting in a chair, or sitting on the floor.
2. For a few beginning minutes, bring gentle awareness to your breath. Feel it fill your lungs and then calmly leave them, only to fill them yet again.
3. Feel yourself breathing in a sense of energy and breathing out apathy. Count these breaths, adding one every time you exhale. In energy, out apathy. Keep up the count until you reach ten full breaths.
4. You are going to go on a mind-journey. Create an image in your mind of a place that feels adventurous. Maybe you've been there before; maybe it's somewhere you've always wanted to go. Fix that image in your mind for a moment.
5. Picture yourself alert and confident, like you can handle anything that your adventure requires. Now, imagine

yourself doing something wild and adventurous. Every time you breathe in, a wave of even more energy enters your body. The day is bright and sunny. You're excited and positive. Embrace your visualization, feeling the air on your skin, the sounds and smells around you. Whatever your adventure is, live it fully!

6. When you are ready, slowly return your breathing to normal, and open your eyes. You can smile if you'd like. Now, take a moment to reflect on how it felt to be on the trip that you created yourself in your own mind:

_____

_____

_____

Abby Confronts a New Reality

The most common examples of bravery are rarely acts of choice. They're acts of necessity, beyond our conscious will.

I can't name exactly what possessed me to reach for my keyboard that evening in late August, heartbroken and fatigued after two weeks at my husband's ICU bedside. I was thirty years old, an elementary school teacher, a new mother to a nearly two-year-old boy. But the only identity I needed the world to know was that I was TC's wife and that I would devote everything to helping him survive the violent assault that had left him with a severe traumatic brain injury.

In those two weeks, every person in my life messaged to ask, "Is he doing better?"

I knew what they didn't: That TC was forever changed. That his disabilities would require him to learn everything anew. That the greatest miracles and the hardest work could not erase the challenges ahead. We would never return to the life we lost.

This was the truth I needed to speak loudly. The night I composed that first blog, the words on the screen before me cemented a reality I was still coping to believe. Life was uncertain, precarious. In this uncharted territory, however, this tender place between life and death, I was learning to see beauty. I used my words to urge others to hold their loved ones tighter, to embrace the precious impermanence of the present moment.

Thousands of readers later, one primitive, personal blog became a formal, published one. A prize-winning essay followed, and then a published book. Two weeks of hospitalization became two months, and then two years of recovery. I wrote it all: the heartaches and joys, the trials that brought me to my knees, the love that became my faith and, ultimately, my will to survive. In telling my truth, I set myself free from the loneliness of heartbreak. In sharing it, I offered others a chance to do the same.

We cannot underestimate the ripple effects of simply choosing to use our voice. It is perhaps our most important act of courage.

Embracing Life's Ninety-Degree Turns

The only people for me are the mad ones, the ones who are mad to live, mad to talk, mad to be saved, desirous of everything at the same time, the ones who never yawn or say a commonplace thing, but burn, burn, burn, like fabulous yellow roman candles exploding like spiders across the stars and in the middle you see the blue centerlight pop and everybody goes "Awww!" —JACK KEROUAC

I love having fellow adventurers in my life. When I feel stymied, they free me. When I feel stuck and unable to express who I really am, they bust me open. When I stray toward wanting a life that is arrow straight, they remind me to embrace the ninety-degree turn.

Ethan Zohn is one of those people.

You may know him as the curly-haired, soccer-playing winner of the third season of CBS's reality show *Survivor* (and its hefty $1 million prize). I happen to know him as a good friend, a Scare Your Soul ambassador, and someone who never fails to lead his life as an unfolding adventure. I happen to know him as someone who sees life as a journey replete with passion and curiosity, fear and tragedy, surprise euphorias, deep darkness, and some totally unplanned ninety-degree turns.

I also happen to know Ethan because, sometimes in life, fate brings two people together at the right time and place. Even under unplanned circumstances.

It was a late Sunday morning in November 2018, and I was late (as usual) on my way to attend a fundraising event at a large convention center. I stepped into the full-capacity event after it had already begun. The lights were down, the room was dark, and a spotlighted emcee was talking on stage. I could see him gesticulating with excitement about the attendance and the guest speaker as I squinted to see table numbers. Stepping on shoes in the dark, I cursed my own lateness, wondering if I would ever find a seat.

A few seconds away from calling it a day and leaving, I saw a good friend—Stacy—waving from a table at the front of the room. Somehow, she had spotted me. I made a beeline, grabbing the only open seat, not knowing that the event's celebrity keynote speaker was sitting beside me.

After the opening remarks, the lights came up and the room settled in to enjoy a brief breakfast before Ethan's speech would begin. Over bagels and coffee, my table-mate Ethan and I chatted.

As happens sometimes in life, it became immediately clear that he and I shared deep values in common. He talked about his passion for encouraging kids around the world to thrive, and I shared my commitment to helping people step into their courageous power. We agreed that we should stay in touch.

Ethan was called to the stage, and I first heard the real story of his life. That speech was stirring.

Ethan grew up in a warm and close Jewish family in Lexington, Massachusetts. He was confident, funny, and did well in school. He was a typical kid with one atypical ability: he had an insane aptitude for soccer. He stood out among his peers. He won awards. He made his family proud. He was on a path.

But when Ethan was fourteen, his dad got sick. It was a horrifically challenging time for Ethan and his family. His father's battle with cancer proved unwinnable, and from this early age, Ethan knew in his bones that life—once thought to be a straight line down a soccer field—could indeed be a very jagged path.

Soccer sustained him. He continued to play through high school and was accepted to Vassar College. While his friends and classmates graduated into jobs and Peace Corps gigs, he took another path.

One that would present another ninety-degree turn.

Based in Bulawayo, Zimbabwe, the Highlanders FC soccer team is one of the most storied in the southern African nation. Founded in 1926, it was originally composed of boys from the local townships. Growing over the years into a local and regional powerhouse, their team proudly maintained their motto: *Siyinqaba!* (We are a fortress!). They were also the team that would welcome the young Jewish man with a jagged path from Massachusetts into their ranks.

With the Highlanders, Ethan would come to love and revere Zimbabwe's history and traditions. From the stage, he told the story of a trip he took into the countryside with a friend. There they came across rows of gravestones, one row on each side of the road. On one side were graves neatly in line, placed on manicured grounds. On the other side, gravestones were nothing more than haphazard piles of crosses and stones. He would later learn that those graves were for the victims of HIV/AIDS. Their sheer number was testament to the impact of the epidemic.

Ethan's eyes were opened and his soul was moved by the experience. He returned to the States, but it wouldn't be long before he was back in Africa.

On a bet with a friend, he submitted an audition tape for a new reality show. Of sixty thousand applicants, only sixteen were selected. And on July 11, 2001, he landed near Kenya's Shaba National Reserve, where he would spend thirty-nine days competing for the *Survivor* crown.

Winning *Survivor* was another ninety-degree turn. Ethan was catapulted into fame. All of a sudden, he was on the cover of magazines and on television. Instead of spending his winnings for material gain, he used a large portion to create a nongovernmental organization—Grassroot Soccer—to help kids around the world in an effort to stem the tide of the scourge that had affected him so much that day in Zimbabwe: HIV and AIDS.

Everything had fallen into place. It was all like a dream.

Until the call came.

It was Ethan's doctor. A swollen lymph node had raised a concern, and the physician had found something. A mass in his chest was the confirmation: he had CD20-positive Hodgkin's lymphoma.

Cancer, the very thief that had stolen his dad, had arrived in his life.

Another ninety-degree turn.

Fame became an irrelevant complication as battling to stay alive took center stage. He underwent treatments, endured the pain and uncertainty, danced daily with his fears. Ethan was happily declared cancer-free in late April 2010, but, twenty months later, cancer returned. He underwent yet another stem-cell transplant, reliving the cycle of pain and fear all over again.

At the time of this publishing, he has been in remission for ten years, and Ethan told us that day that his experiences—the greatest challenges—were what fueled his advocating for AIDS education, empowering young people struggling with cancer, and using sports and his public spotlight for social good.

After speaking, Ethan returned to his seat. Something had shifted in the room. We were all experiencing the elasticity of liberation, the communal knowing that life will never be without the ninety-degree turns that create the adventurous journey of our lives.

Writing Prompt: Exploring Uncertainty and Your Own Ninety-Degree Turns

Reflect on one "ninety-degree turn" that had an unforgettable impact on you. What happened and how did it change your life?

_____

_____

_____

_____

_____

_____

Memory Glue

> Everybody needs his memories. They keep the wolf of insignificance from the door. —SAUL BELLOW

You may not have heard of Cesare Pavese, but you probably know one of his quotes by heart.

Pavese was one of Italy's most celebrated twentieth-century authors. He was the winner of the Strega Prize—his country's most prestigious literary award—and the author of more than a dozen novels and short stories. Pavese's diary was discovered after his death in 1950, and in it, someone happened upon this quote: "We don't remember days. We remember moments."

To illustrate this, I'll introduce you to Marilu Henner.

The actress is best known for her role on the late-1970s-era sitcom *Taxi*. But her memory is what's rightfully astounding. Possessing an uncommon ability known as hyperthymesia, Henner can recall every single day of her adult life with amazing clarity.

Take, randomly, April 30, 1980: "It was a Wednesday," she said in a *Brain & Life* magazine interview. "I was in Cancun, Mexico, with my boyfriend at the time, who was soon to be my first husband.... The weather was beautiful that night, but it poured rain the next day, and all the plumbing in our resort went out. The whole thing comes back. It's like remembering your address or phone number or the color of your eyes. It's just there."[6]

For 99.9 percent of us, days seamlessly blend from one to the next, blurring so much that sometimes we don't even remember the year in which a certain event occurred. We forget that we even have a routine, and day by day we sleepwalk through our lives. Weeks become months; months become years. Sometimes, we're reminded of certain things—from old photos or conversations—and think, *Where has the time gone? It seems like yesterday!*

Our lives speed by, and we forget their minutiae. But we don't forget our adventures.

It's all about our neurochemistry. When we have adventures, adrenaline is released throughout our bodies. And new research by James McGaugh, professor of neurobiology at the

University of California at Irvine, reveals that adrenaline is the glue for long-term memory, helping us remember better. Those experiences—our adventures—are sealed in. So, when we begin to lead our daily lives like adventures, we begin to carry those rich memories with us.[7]

We capture Cesare Pavese's moments like a camera.

Scare Your Soul Challenge: Create Your Adventure Plan

Now that we've explored the role of adventure in your life, it's time to move into reflection and action.

Part I: Reflections

Reflection one: What is the "wildest" thing you've ever done? (Define that however you would like!) Take a few minutes to write about it in glorious detail. If you'd like, share with a friend who knew you at the time.

_____

_____

_____

_____

_____

Reflection two: What "adventurer" has inspired you, and what do you love about their style or attitude on life? Maybe it's someone you read about or someone you know personally. (This doesn't have to be someone who others would see as an "adventurer"—as you know, there are many ways to define _adventure._)

_____

_____

_____

Part II: Actions

Action one: In the next two weeks, what is one adventure you will take within a hundred feet of your own front door?

_____

_____

_____

Action two: Find an adventure partner and agree on a destination or experience that would be "adventurous" to you both. Open your mind as to what this could be for you. Choose something that is safe but feels boundary pushing.

_____

_____

_____

Key Insights

1. Leading a life of adventure does not mean traveling to climb the Acropolis or gaze at the northern lights. It means looking at our own lives with a sense of wonder, of novelty. Every single day provides an opportunity to see the world with fresh eyes.

2. A key to leading an adventurous life is navigating the "ninety-degree turns"—the unexpected challenges and opportunities. It is in our ability to take the corners with openness that we experience the fullness of life.

3. Adventure imparts a delicious sense of uncertainty. "Getting lost" allows us to experience a moment's serendipity, eschewing the cloying common sense that we must have complete control over our routines.

4. Memories are the currency of a life well lived, and living with a sense of adventure seals in memory. When we stay in our comfort zones, life tends to fly by, melding one day into the next.

5. Keeping an attitude of adventure close at mind and heart ensures we live fully in the present, creating and solidifying memories for the future.

CHAPTER 10

Courage Principle Three: Energy

Energy and persistence conquer all things.

—BENJAMIN FRANKLIN

Jesse Harless—bald with glasses, good-looking—bounded into the coffeehouse and shook my hand heartily. Our mutual friend, a beautiful curly-haired yoga instructor and musician named Marni, had suggested that we meet while Jesse was in town. But it was what she said about him that really piqued my interest: "He's a cold-shower expert," she informed me.

Now, full disclosure: I love a hot shower. It is where I do my best thinking, it is where I can relax, it's my escape from the pulls and pushes of daily life. Interrupting that joyous experience with a blast of cold water? Why?

I needed to understand.

Like me, Jesse had grown up plagued by self-doubt, shyness, and social anxiety.

His early high school years started with a sense of promise, but addictive behaviors like pornography and online gaming—which temporarily numbed his fear and anxiety—diverted him from a healthy path. The loss of a loved one affected him deeply, prompting him to try cocaine, which he then became addicted to for years. Soon after, he would discover heroin.

Jesse hit rock bottom when a huge cache of illegal opioid pills arrived in the mail. Federal agents were waiting.

Threatened with the possibility of years in prison, he decided it was time to clean up. He launched into an intensive recovery process that included journaling, 12-step programs, and daily affirmations. But his feelings of self-worth remained low. One day, a friend suggested that he try a simple program: one cold shower a day for thirty days.

A cold shower? How could that possibly make an impact?

"I stayed in that cold shower for a full five minutes," he told me. "I emerged and would never be the same again. For the next three hours, I felt incredible energy and excitement—a level of energy I had never experienced before."

From that day forward, Jesse has taken a cold shower every morning without skipping a day. He explained more about the health benefits, the discipline it provided, the role it had in his ongoing addiction recovery—and importantly, the vast amounts of energy it fostered.

After ten minutes of listening to his story, I was "in." I suggested that we create a weeklong Scare Your Soul challenge promoting cold showers. And just like every other challenge, I would join our participants and do it myself.

"Start slowly," Jesse counseled. "Start with cold water only at the end of a hot shower and increase the length every day."

So, on that first day, after my normal morning shower, I nervously turned the dial all the way to the right. I'm glad I was alone in my bathroom because my reaction was embarrassing.

I swore, hopped up and down, flung the freezing water back and forth across my scalp in some vain attempt to shed the cold. I couldn't catch my breath. After thirty seconds, I stopped the insanity and stepped out of the shower. I felt...well...*amazing*. I felt warm, happy, proud of myself for this tiny accomplishment.

But more than anything, I felt energized.

It All Starts with Energy

Great ideas originate in the muscles.

—THOMAS EDISON

Dan Buettner is a whirlwind of positive, health-conscious energy.

He is a world traveler, a National Geographic Fellow, and an award-winning journalist and speaker. But he is probably most well-known for his groundbreaking work in studying human longevity around the world. His research led to a 2005 *National Geographic* cover story entitled, "The Secrets of Living Longer," and two follow-up books focusing on "Blue Zones."

Blue Zones, as defined by Buettner, are the five places in the world—Okinawa, Japan; Sardinia, Italy; Nicoya, Costa Rica; Ikaria, Greece; and Loma Linda, California—where people live the longest. Their behavior, diet, and lifestyle habits fuel a life full of energy, meaning, and good health.

Buettner's research inspired what Scare Your Soul calls its "Energy Week."

It is all about courageously supercharging the energy we need to grow, to connect, and to maintain our health: all of the things we need to live a courageous life.

We all know how we feel when we are burnt out, depleted, out of energy. Everything in our life, especially the hard and challenging things, falls by the wayside. Apathy sets in. We lose our edge. We set in motion a downward spiral of bad habits and low energy. But when we courageously tackle key habits, we supercharge our body and mind for the courageous work ahead. In our Scare Your Soul energy week, we focus on seven:

1. Get mindful (cultivating presence)
2. Get sweaty with a friend (movement and social connection)

3. Take a cold shower (optimizing the body/mind connection)
4. Learn something new (activate our essential curiosity to learn)
5. Simplify (focus on our core essentials, not our stuff)
6. Get spiritual (energize our transcendent selves)
7. Take a break (rest and regenerate)

Alan Seale, my former coach and the founder of the Center for Transformational Presence, would constantly remind me that we all have a finite amount of energy to expend each day. Think of water rushing through a garden hose: The key is to get as much water through the hose and minimize the number of small holes in the hose that send the water flying in other directions. You want as much water/energy as possible directed where you need it.

Ensuring that we have as much energy as possible—and direct it exactly where it will benefit us the most—is what this week is about.

It will be scary. It will be worth it.

I promise.

Your Energized Week

> Every day, think as you wake up, today I am fortunate to be alive. I have a precious human life, I am not going to waste it.
>
> —HIS HOLINESS THE 14TH DALAI LAMA

In this chapter, we will spend one week—Sunday to Saturday (or a weeklong stretch that's convenient for you)—focused on actions that will supercharge us. The goal is to help us amp up our feelings of being alive, focused, creative, and alert.

And at the end, you'll have a whole range of new memories and experiences from which to form new energizing rituals.

Here are a few key guiding principles for your energized week:

Consider this week your "screen detox." Reduce all news and social media consumption to zero. This will take incredible discipline, but it is a crucial step to your success. You can do it!

Understand the power of small actions. At first blush, you may wonder, *One week? How could that possibly make a difference in my life?* The answer is this: small acts are proven to make nearly as much of an effect as major ones. The key, as with every chapter in this book, is to *do them*. They are designed for impact.

Prepare in advance and modify if necessary. Plan ahead and you'll set yourself up for success:

- Set a journal or pad of paper and a pen next to your bed.
- Read the entire week's plan first so you know what's coming.
- If possible, clean out your bedroom of anything that isn't directly related to sleep (put your TV remote in a drawer and place devices in another room).
- If, for some reason, you need to swap one activity for another go right ahead. The key is to make sure you cover all seven major activities in the week.

Rally your allies. Let your family and friends know that you are spending this week differently, so they can support you. Even better: invite a friend, spouse, or child to join you for this week's courageous activities.

Setting the Baseline

As you begin the week, take your emotional, physical, and mental temperature. For each question, place a circle around the number based on how you are feeling right now—at this moment—with 1 being the lowest score and 10 being the highest:

1. How would you rate your overall level of happiness?

   1—2—3—4—5—6—7—8—9—10

2. How courageous are you feeling in life overall?

   1—2—3—4—5—6—7—8—9—10

3. How would you rate your overall energy level?

   1—2—3—4—5—6—7—8—9—10

4. How "on track" do you feel in living your desired life?

   1—2—3—4—5—6—7—8—9—10

Add up your total score and write it here: _____

The Week Ahead

Each day, you have the opportunity to experience consistent morning and evening rituals, as outlined here:

Morning Rituals, Days One through Seven

1. Set your alarm to wake you before sunrise.
2. Write for five minutes using the daily wake-up prompt.
3. Get calm and clear, and enjoy watching the sunrise.

Evening Rituals, Days One through Seven

1. Set an early bedtime in advance—one that works with your schedule. Plan on at least seven hours of sleep (if not more).
2. Turn off all devices an hour before bedtime and place them in another room.
3. Lay out clothes and any other items you will need for the next day so you don't have to think about them in the morning.
4. Write for five minutes using your evening prompt right before bed.

Day One: Get Mindful

Meditation is the ultimate mobile device; you can use it anywhere, anytime, unobtrusively. —SHARON SALZBERG

Wake-up writing prompt: *When you are alone in your thoughts, what do you feel? What takes up the mental geography in your head?*

_____

_____

_____

Today's goal: The practice of *meditation* is an uncomfortable one for many. Let go of preconceptions. If you are a meditation beginner, today is about just breathing and being present. If you are more experienced, it is about cultivating your "beginner's mind." Pick a time, before or after sunrise, and find a quiet and comfortable place. Set a timer for ten minutes.

1. Sit with as straight a spine as you can. Take several deep breaths in and out to calm your mind, and then breathe normally.
2. Pay attention. Feel the air coming into your nostrils (can you feel the change in temperature at the tip of your nose?) and then filling up your lungs.
3. Now, shift your focus to wherever your breath feels the strongest: your nose, your lungs, your belly. And just be. When you get lost or spun out in a thought or fantasy (which you absolutely will), just bring your attention back to the breath. Your only job is to stay present in the moment.
4. After the ten minutes, take one long, deep breath.
5. During the course of the rest of the day, try to remember the feeling of presence and focus. Pay attention to your

surroundings. Return to focusing on your breath when you need a vehicle for feeling present.

Why it's courageous: Many of us find mindfulness work to be the most challenging aspect of all of the contemplative practices.

- We feel like we are "failing" when our minds wander.
- We are not used to just sitting and being present. We crave distraction.
- We are so attuned to getting "results" from an effort. Mindfulness is a process.
- We are afraid that someone will interrupt us or we will feel foolish.

Why it works: Mindfulness is being fully present and aware of where we are and what we're doing and not being overly reactive or overwhelmed by what's going on around us. The practice has evolved significantly from its early days as a traditional Buddhist concept, and its health benefits have been and are being studied widely. Countless research studies over the years have shown that mindfulness meditation can have a positive impact on a huge range of health conditions, including alleviating post-traumatic stress disorder, protecting the brain from aging, decreasing stress, and improving concentration and mental clarity.

Evening writing prompt: *Describe the feeling of meditating and being present. Was it calming, frustrating, liberating?*

Energizing Day Two: Get Sweaty with a Friend

It is exercise alone that supports these spirits, and keeps the mind in vigor. —CICERO

Wake-up writing prompt: *What is your favorite type of exercise? What about it makes you love it? What could you do to help yourself do it just 10 percent more per month?*

_____

_____

_____

Today's goal: Exercise for at least thirty minutes, intentionally trying something new and inviting a friend to join you.

Your ultimate goal is to try a new physical exercise you've never done before (how about one you are intimidated to try?). Perhaps it's taking an online yoga class, going for a run, or visiting a boxing gym. Be bold. Take a walk in the sunshine if that is what is available to you and within your ability.

The most important thing is to get your body moving, get your heart rate up, and invite a friend or loved one to join you. Experience it together and take time to connect.

Why it's courageous: We can get into a comfort zone physically just as easily as any other aspect of our lives. We fall into habits, taking the same classes or repeating the same exercise patterns; or worse, we don't exercise at all. We project all kinds of possible outcomes: we might get injured, we'll be sore, we don't know what we are doing, we will look silly or incompetent, we will feel bad about ourselves.

Why it works: Exercise is consistently the single best way to quickly increase our energy level. It is recommended across the board for all ages and is the number one predictor of good health throughout all phases of life. Physical activity triggers your body to produce more mitochondria—which create fuel from the food you eat and oxygen from the air you breathe—inside your muscle cells. Exercise boosts oxygen circulation inside the body, increases hormone levels that make us more energized, and much more.

We get a double benefit when we exercise with other people, strengthening social bonds, getting a boost of hormones from the interaction, and focusing less on the hardship of vigorous exercise since we are "doing it together."

Evening writing prompt: *When you drift off to sleep tonight, what is one thing you will be proud of?*

_____

_____

_____

Energizing Day Three: Take a Cold Shower

But, there is still every reason for healthy people to take cold showers, or swim outside in cold water. It gives you the feeling that you are alive. —WIM HOF

Wake-up writing prompt: *"Waking up" can mean more than just the transition of consciousness from sleep to wakefulness. What parts of your life do you feel like you are sleepwalking through?*

_____

_____

_____

Today's goal: It's simple: in the last thirty seconds of your hot shower, turn the dial to the coldest temperature possible.

Why it's courageous: Most of us would probably say yes to participating in some sort of polar plunge for charity every year or so, but the thought of subjecting our bodies to a torrent of cold water in our own shower is a tough sell. Yes, the experience can be physically challenging in the moment, but most of the "pain" here comes from us *thinking* about how the experience will be rather than just trying it out for ourselves.

Why it works: Cold water immersion (CWI) is a form of cold water therapy that helps your nervous system manage stress better and helps you build confidence and willpower. The positive effects are many; here are just a few:

- **Improved mood and energy:** Cold showers can reduce heart rate, lower blood pressure, and release endorphins that can help with our overall mood and energy level.
- **Enhanced circulation:** Your body's lymphatic system is a network of vessels that remove waste, bacteria, and microbes; CWI causes those vessels to contract, forcing the lymphatic system to pump more lymph fluids throughout the body, flushing out waste and kicking our immune system into gear.
- **Reduced muscle inflammation:** We've all felt that "day after" soreness in our muscles that comes from an especially hard or new exercise, and we've seen athletes taking an ice bath after a game or workout. Known as delayed-onset muscle soreness (DOMS), it is due to microscopic tears in the fibers and inflammation in muscle tissue. CWI helps counteract DOMS by lowering the damaged tissue's temperature and constricting blood vessels, reducing swelling and inflammation, and even numbing nerve endings to bring immediate relief.
- **Positive impact on our sense of resolve:** Taking a cold shower often fosters a powerful positive feeling of "doing something hard but healthy" first thing in the morning. We begin our day energized and feeling good about our discipline.

Evening writing prompt: *What impact did the cold shower have on you today? Do you feel more "awake" in life in any way because of it?*

_____

_____

_____

Energizing Day Four: Learn Something New

Learning is a treasure that will follow its owner everywhere.

—CHINESE PROVERB

Wake-up writing prompt: *What is one thing you've always wanted to learn about?*

_____

_____

_____

Today's goal: In a small, actionable way, take steps to start learning one new thing you didn't know before. It could be something you've always been curious about and truly wanted to learn, or it could be more arbitrary (even random). Don't feel pressure to do it all in one day; if it is something big you've always wanted to do, take the first step.

If something doesn't come to mind immediately, try one of these: cook one new recipe, learn ten words in a language you've never even considered, read or watch something about the history of a country or city or style of architecture you've always driven by and not stopped to think about.

Why it's courageous: It can feel scary to be the beginner, to not possess knowledge about something or feel even a small sense of mastery. What can happen when we learn something completely new? It's risky! We can fail at it, we can feel dumb or embarrassed, it can remind us that there is so much about the world that we ourselves don't yet know.

Why it works: Learning enlivens us. Our brains buzz with dopamine when we encounter an exciting new thought or technique. We gain a sense of positivity and pride when we take even a small action toward learning something new. New ideas make us happier, create more connections between our existing pieces of knowledge of the world, and make us more interesting.

Evening writing prompt: *What did you learn today that you didn't know yesterday? If you had to teach someone else about this newfound knowledge, what would you say?*

_____

_____

_____

Energizing Day Five: Simplify

> Things do not change, we change. Sell your clothes and keep your thoughts. —HENRY DAVID THOREAU

Wake-up writing prompt: *What is the one material item in your home that was expensive to buy but holds little value to you now? Why?*

_____

_____

_____

Today's goal: Consider an aspect of your home or work life that feels cluttered and, to be blunt, get rid of it. That may mean ruthlessly getting down to zero emails in your inbox, cleaning out your closet and packing up 50 percent of it to give to charity or dispose of responsibly, or decluttering those chipped dishes or ancient TV remotes. You don't need to tackle your whole house or office in one day; just choose one area and get it done.

Why it's courageous: Within our inherent nature is a desire to fill holes in our hearts or psyches.

Sometimes we do that with gratitude, human connection, acts of giving, spirituality, and charity. And sometimes, in moments of disconnection, we fill those holes through so-called retail therapy, coveting the newest gadget or item of clothing or whatever piques our interest. But those items—whether we like it or not—most often end up as junk, weighing down our minds just like they do our closets. Sometimes getting rid of old items feels like giving away our history; the truth is, the history lies in your memories, not in the old toys your children don't play with anymore or the clothes you no longer wear.

Why it works: Clutter actually affects our mood and self-esteem. Clutter increases cortisol levels in our bodies, leading to feelings of stress and other negative mental states. The pile of unwashed laundry, the dolls littering the kitchen floor, and the disorganized closets busting at the seams are literally and figuratively weighing us down. Simplifying gives us a sense of lightness and accomplishment, not to mention the psychological boost that comes from donating our used items to those who will give them new life.

Evening writing prompt: *You are being sent to another planet to live and the basics will be provided. You can bring one personal item with you. What is it, and why?*

_____

_____

_____

Energizing Day Six: Get Spiritual

> Your sacred space is where you can find yourself over and over again. —JOSEPH CAMPBELL

Wake-up writing prompt: *Recount one time when you completely lost sense of yourself—when you were so engrossed in something that you forgot about your own worries, deadlines, duties, your own sense of individual self for a time.*

_____

_____

_____

Today's goal: Today is all about connecting with something beyond our own minds and bodies. Spiritual energy—whether we tap into it through a religious experience, an appreciation of nature, art, or music, or a mind-expanding moment that reminds us that we are connected to something greater than ourselves—is a powerful energizer. Today, find one way to express your spirituality that is meaningful for you. Really embrace it:

- Attend a faith or religious service (or find one online and feel like you are there)
- Read a text that is spiritual to you, whether it is something familiar or completely new
- Teach one spiritual concept you care about to a child
- Spend time in nature, drinking in the experience and giving thanks
- Give back in some way, whether it is through an hour of volunteering or giving back to a neighbor selflessly

Why it's courageous: An introspective practice encourages a sense of humility, of grace. This places the responsibility on us to delve into that experience, not as others might, but as only we uniquely can in the moment. As author, Buddhist monk, and meditation teacher Jack Kornfield writes,

The spiritual path does not present us with a prescribed, pat formula for everyone to follow. It is not a matter of imitation. We cannot be Mother Teresa or Gandhi or the Buddha. We have to be ourselves. We must discover and connect with our unique expression of the truth. We must learn to listen to and trust ourselves.[1]

Why it works: Experiences of transcendence are beneficial in so many ways. They connect us to meaning, they put our petty wants and hurts in perspective, they amp up our gratitude, they make us feel that we have more time. All of this spiritual housecleaning liberates our minds, lowers cortisol levels, makes us feel unbound and magnanimous.

And we are just beginning to see how spirituality affects stress levels and body mechanics; one Harvard study confirmed that Tibetan monks in deep spiritual meditation could increase their own core body temperatures for extended periods of time.

Evening writing prompt: *Describe the spiritual connection that you made today. Do you want more of it in your life, and if so, how would you do that?*

_____

_____

_____

Energizing Day Seven: Take a Break

The meaning of life is just to be alive. It is so plain and so obvious and so simple. And yet, everybody rushes around in a great panic as if it were necessary to achieve something beyond themselves. —ALAN WATTS

Wake-up writing prompt: *What in life is better with less effort rather than more effort?*

_____

Today's goal: Clear your calendar. Read, take a nap, take a walk. Let your body and mind relax.

Why it's courageous: For some, this may be the week's most challenging goal. Most of us feel overwhelmed and too busy; in many cases, we create that reality, generating busyness to distract ourselves. We overpromise to make others happy with us, we over-schedule so we don't have to confront sadness or ennui, we get wedded to our rituals with no chance to actually relax and reflect. Our culture tells us we should be on our laptops, not in the woods. Author Alex Soojung-Kim Pang writes, "When we treat workaholics as heroes, we express a belief that labor rather than contemplation is the wellspring of great ideas and that the success of individuals and companies is a measure of their long hours."[2]

Why it works: Rest and regeneration are critical to high-functioning human beings. Just as our muscles need the time to repair, our minds need space to reflect. Rest reduces stress, enhances creativity, improves our productivity, magnifies our ability to make optimal decisions, boosts our immune systems, increases our level of patience, slows down the aging process, and so much more.

Evening writing prompt: *With the week wrapping up, take some time to describe the impact. What made the greatest change to your overall level of energy? What made this week meaningful and important to you?*

Maria Fills the Bag, Bean by Bean

Mom used to say, "Bean by bean fills the bag." Something I was seriously considering as I stood at the foot of Mount Kilimanjaro, the fourth highest peak in the world.

I had never climbed a mountain or trained to climb one. I was just finishing an eight-month project in Tanzania. Someone on my team was a mountaineer and offered to take those interested to the summit. Impulsively, I raised my hand and now was about to take my first step into the unknown. I did not know if I could keep up with the group, how I would do at altitude, or, most of all, how I would deal with my fear of heights.

Compounding my anxiety was that for the last several months, I had been everyone's boss. I felt ashamed to show even the slightest hint of fear. So we began our six-day journey. I soon learned if I simply followed the shoe heel in front of me rather than look up the mountain, I could get through that day.

"Bean by bean," I climbed.

Then came the moment we had to scramble over Barranco Wall, the steepest section. While we were making our way across the wall, everyone said, "Look at the view!"

I replied, "I will look when I get to the top," as I just watched my hands reaching for the next stone to hoist myself up onto.

When we got to camp that night, I admitted my fear of heights. That confession brought a round of applause and encouraging support from the others for the rest of our climb. It made the eventual summit all the more euphoric. That experience gave me the confidence to try other daring things and taught me to be OK with being vulnerable.

People who love you will be there for you.

Revisiting Your Baseline

As you end the week, take a moment to revisit your baseline—your emotional, physical, and mental temperature you took earlier in the chapter. For each question, answer based on how you are feeling right now—at this moment—with 1 being the lowest score and 10 being the highest:

1. How would you rate your overall level of happiness?

   1—2—3—4—5—6—7—8—9—10

   Difference (+/–) vs. your previous baseline: _____

2. How courageous are you feeling in life overall?

   1—2—3—4—5—6—7—8—9—10

   Difference (+/–) vs. your previous baseline: _____

3. How would you rate your overall energy level?

   1—2—3—4—5—6—7—8—9—10

   Difference (+/–) vs. your previous baseline: _____

4. How "on track" do you feel in living your desired life?

   1—2—3—4—5—6—7—8—9—10

   Difference (+/–) vs. your previous baseline: _____

Keeping the Energy Flowing

My sincere hope is that this week was rife with new experiences, happy surprises, a sense of clarity, and most specifically, renewed energy for the journey. Which begs the questions: Which of this week's practices felt the most powerful to you? Which ones do you want to continue as part of your life?

Take a moment to reflect, and list four things that you want to carry forward:

1. _____

2. _____

3. _____

4. _____

As we conclude this experience of small acts, remember that a fulfilling life isn't made up of the grand gestures and big leaps into the abyss, but of the small, hour-by-hour choices that we make.

Key Insights

1. Energy supercharges our bodies and minds, giving us the needed forward motion into the lives we want. Without rituals and strategies—many of which take time, attention, and courage—we can be left depleted and burnt out.

2. Our lack of sleep, excessive screen time, mental burden from the news and curated social media feeds, lack of exercise, and little time for rest all conspire to deprive us of the energy we need to thrive.

3. The goal is to engage in positive, science-based, courageous activities that energize us. A mindfulness practice, exercise (especially with a friend), cold water therapy, learning something new, simplifying our surroundings, engaging in a spiritual pursuit, and taking time for rest all contribute to an energized life.

4. This Scare Your Soul week is designed to be a tasting menu of small, positive interventions. Layered over a foundation of good sleep, reduced screen time, awe-inducing

experiences, and social interaction, it will provide you with the tools you need—and enjoy using—that you can carry forward into your life. Each intervention is meant to be doable quickly, and time for reflection and writing is essential for its success.

CHAPTER 11

Courage Principle Four: Curiosity

Flourishing is not a solo endeavor.

—BARBARA FREDRICKSON

Curiosity fosters connection...and connection unlocks joy.

That thought made its way into my mind as I sat at my favorite coffeehouse's long communal table, laptop open. The burnt caramel scent of roasted coffee beans wafted through the air.

Scare Your Soul was just a few months old, and time was running short to debut our first real shared challenge for our growing list of "soulsters."

Scare Your Soul's kickoff—a weekend of comfort zone–pushing activities—had exceeded all of my expectations. I watched from my computer screen as people across the globe signed up for this fledgling movement, tackling their fears and sharing their successes with each other. Now it was time to progress. I wanted to offer a simple act, relatively easy and inexpensive to do, that would provide our participants with a rush of healthy anxiety and that could be shared with even more people around the world. It needed to embody the factors that were our secret sauce: ease, healthy nervousness, and shareability.

But I just could not come up with it.

Every few minutes, I'd look up from my laptop, watching a line of yet-to-be-caffeinated patrons, phones in hand, snaking around the coffee bar. Heads down, oblivious to the people around them, pecking and scrolling.

And then it hit me.

What if the challenge was to offer to buy a cup of coffee for a stranger in a coffee shop or restaurant and, while waiting for it to arrive, engage in a short but meaningful conversation? It felt simple and actionable. It got people off their phones and sparked connection.

Equally important, it had an air of scary uncertainty. You wouldn't know what would happen unless you took the risk. I looked down at my own empty mug, stood up, and went to test out my new idea. As I joined the back of the line and people began filing in behind me, I felt that sense of creeping anxiety.

Whom should I ask? What exactly do I say? What if they get the wrong idea... or refuse? What if they are offended, or if this causes a scene?

Even the smallest human interactions that fall outside our comfort zone can rattle us, and as I snuck a glance ahead of me (at an older man in a blue puffer jacket and an orange cap) and behind me (at a woman in a long, dark coat with a hospital name badge clipped to its lapel), I felt the rattle. Yep, exactly what I wanted.

"Hello, I'm Scott," I said to the woman. "I'm a participant in the Scare Your Soul courage movement, and today I'm challenging myself to buy a cup of coffee for a stranger. So... would it be OK if I bought you a coffee?"

I was greeted with a smile.

"Hell yes, you can!"

Her name was Marcia, and she and I talked for the next five minutes as we waited for our coffees. She told me about her new grandchild (named Summer), her plans for the weekend (working in her yard if it got warm enough or visiting a friend if it didn't), and what she did professionally (she was a nurse in the OB-GYN practice at a local hospital).

"So, what's your favorite part of your job?" I asked her.

"Helping to bring those beautiful babies into this world," Marcia said without hesitation.

She took her coffee with half-and-half. She told me that this experience had absolutely made her day. The barista behind the counter, overhearing our conversation, said the same and joyously comped the coffees. Others in line smiled. Marcia gave me a hug.

As I got in my car later, I felt like I had been jump-started by some kind of strange electrical current. I felt brave (odd, given such a small act) and generous (bizarre, given that I hadn't even paid a penny). I immediately called a few of our new Scare Your Soul ambassadors to tell them about my experience, and they jumped at the chance to do it, too. For the rest of the day, I received updates of people buying coffee for others around the world. I saw the ripples of impact.

I saw the gem of a larger potential.

The key, I would come to learn, was that taking risks to further human connection is a powerful and liberating act. We humans are social animals, and it can sometimes take a brave act—an outstretched hand, an open ear—to really achieve connection.

When we fixate on obstacles like our fear of others, of the unknown, of social interactions—not to mention getting stuck in our narcissistic bubbles of phone scrolling, constant texting, or the heavily curated social and political networks we may find ourselves in—it becomes harder to fill that basic human need for connection. In addition, in the context of a polarized world, where we don't know the political beliefs of the stranger on the bus next to us, or where an unseen virus can mean that any individual has the potential to do us harm, we can become relationally starved.

The impact of this is significant. We miss out on the energizing joy of small connection. We miss out on meeting the gem of a human being standing right next to us. When we let fear of failure or the unknown creep into our lives, we avoid the necessary tough conversations at work or home. We don't defend our new ideas when they are challenged by the status quo. We hold our tongue in the face of injustice.

The "coffee and conversation" challenge I designed that day was just a taste, though it has become a Scare Your Soul favorite. Yes, there have been uncomfortable and unpleasant moments along the way. One time in particular, a man became irate at one of our Scare Your Soul ambassadors in a San Diego coffee shop, ranting at full volume in front of everyone before finally storming out. But the vast majority of the experiences brought small—and not-so-small—moments of courage and connection. Here are just a few:

- One conversation led the Scare Your Soul participant to find that she and her coffee beneficiary both worked in marketing and had earned their MBAs from the same university (in different decades). They are now business partners.
- One conversation about tattoos (the participant had none, and her beneficiary was a tattoo artist) inspired the participant to leave the coffee shop and go directly to her new friend's tattoo parlor. She got a tattoo of her twins' names on her ankle...and was not charged a penny.
- One conversation led a Southern California participant to find that she and the woman behind her were from the same small town in Michigan and that their mothers were friends. Together they called their very surprised moms from the Starbucks.

Scare Your Soul Challenge: Engage in "Coffee and Conversation"

Visit a coffee shop or restaurant. Without too much planning, offer to buy a stranger a coffee or tea while you're there. If you'd prefer, you can mention that you are part of a courage challenge or that you're working on your own expression of bravery in social situations, and that you hope that they will allow you to get this for them. If they don't agree, find a time during the day to do something similar with another stranger; if they do agree (and hopefully they will), take the time to engage in a short but curious conversation. Ask open-ended questions, with a goal of eliciting information about that person that surprises, delights, or interests. Share something about yourself.

Congrats on taking this first step! There's a lot more to come. Take some time to write down the experience. How did the coffee challenge feel before, during, and after? Any takeaways?

_____

_____

_____

Honey and Trombones

> You make me feel like honey and trombones.
>
> —ANIS MOJGANI

When I speak to audiences about happiness and courage, I will often tell them that I am going to show them—via my PowerPoint presentation—a photo of someone who may possibly know more about happiness than *anyone else alive*. Encouraging them to throw out guesses on who I might be referring to, I see the hands rise quickly:

"The Dalai Lama."

"Deepak Chopra."

"Gretchen Rubin."

Then I share a photo of a kind-looking, unassuming gentleman, easily in his late sixties, with sandy-brown hair, wearing a light-blue dress shirt. Even after I tell the audience that his TED Talk has been viewed over 41 million times, only once did someone correctly identify Bob Waldinger. "The guy who leads that Harvard happiness study, right?"

Bob is a professor of psychiatry at Harvard Medical School, a psychoanalyst, and a Zen priest, who, indeed, leads the Harvard Study of Adult Development, one of the longest-running studies of all time.

Launched in 1938, the study began by tracking the health of 268 Harvard sophomores in hopes of revealing clues as to what constitutes a happy, healthy life. Scientists eventually expanded the cohort to include the offspring of the original group, and now, eighty-three years after it began, the study has data from more than two thousand people, represents four generations, and boasts the lowest dropout rate (15 percent) of any long-term study in history.

The study has produced data that has spawned hundreds of scientific papers and several books, but there is one single clarion call that supersedes all others: the revelation that the happiest, most successful people aren't the ones with the largest bank accounts or highest IQs. They are the ones that have the strongest social relationships.

"When we gathered together everything we knew about them at about age fifty, it wasn't their middle-age cholesterol levels that predicted how they were going to grow old," he said in his now-famous TED Talk. "It was how satisfied they were in their relationships. The people who were the most satisfied in their relationships at age fifty were the healthiest at age eighty."[1]

And the lesson didn't end there. The importance of these relationships, research tells us, is not the quantity but the quality. The defining factor was the *depth of connection.*

And the power of social connection isn't just seen in the statistics. In 2017, surgeon general Dr. Vivek Murthy told the *Washington Post*, "When you look at the data, what's really interesting is loneliness has been found to be associated with a reduction of life span. The reduction in life span [for loneliness] is similar to that caused by smoking 15 cigarettes a day."[2]

We all want connection that quells loneliness and sadness and that leads to the kind of deep, loving, courageous, vulnerable, amazing lives we deserve. We all want love. To put it more poetically, we all want people around us that make us feel, as poet Anis Mojgani writes, "like honey and trombones."[3]

Money, Sex, and Roller Coasters

> Everybody, everybody everywhere, has his own movie going, his own scenario, and everybody is acting his movie out like mad.... —TOM WOLFE

Curiosity is a superhighway to connection.

When we direct our interest to really trying to understand others—their background, their motivations, their insecurities, their positions—we create connection and intimacy.

I have a friend, Stuart, who is by far the most curious person I've ever known. His interest in other people is insatiable. He is that person whom you can find at a party, in the corner, deep in conversation with someone he didn't know when he stepped through the front door. By the time he leaves, he will know insanely detailed items about that person: what they love to do, how they feel about global politics, what their favorite Indian restaurant is, and where they had their first kiss. It's no surprise that people absolutely *love* Stuart.

So, what is happening in Stuart's brain as he is having these conversations? Let's tack back to curiosity's origins.

Curiouser and Curiouser

> Curiosity is the lust of the mind. —THOMAS HOBBES

Many researchers believe that curiosity arose within us as a survival instinct: to thrive in an uncertain and dangerous world, our ancestors needed to know about the environment around them—

topography, weather, weapons and implements, the predators and prey around them. Evolutionarily, therefore, curiosity became part of our survival tool kit. And biologically, it has remained a powerful force.

Curiosity lights up our brains in many of the same ways that money, sex, and roller coasters do.

Studies conducted throughout the scientific world have utilized MRIs to measure the impact of curiosity. In one conducted at the University of California, Davis, participants were shown one hundred trivia questions and then asked to rate how curious they were about the answer to each question. Then their brain activity and their sense of recall were measured; the questions that elicited the most initial curiosity were the ones that spurred the highest brain activity, and subsequently, the participants were able to better recall those questions and answers even days after the experiment.

The MRI scans also showed a boost in activity in the hippocampus, the part of our limbic system that regulates our emotions and stores our memories.[4] When we're curious, our brains also release dopamine, the neurotransmitter that is delivered when we feel something pleasurable.

All the powerful effects of curiosity can be used to foster strong and healthy relationships. The interaction we see and feel when someone is interested in us—from the earliest of ages—has been proven to have a significant impact.

In the mid-1970s, Edward Tronick and his colleagues were intrigued about how variations in interest in another—as seen through facial expressions—might impact the psyche of a child. In groundbreaking work, called the "still-face experiment," a mother sat face-to-face with her one-year-old child, cooing, laughing, and smiling. She showed curiosity in her expression and through her words when her child made a face or pointed. It's something we've likely experienced any time we've interacted with a child.

But then the mother was directed by Tronick's team to turn her head away for a moment and then back, this time maintaining a plaintive, flat response. No smiling, no laughing, and no curiosity. The impact was dramatic and unsettling. The child noticed the change immediately, acting at first confused and then agitated. She tried repeated attempts to gain curious attention before dissolving into tears of hopelessness. *All of this happened in less than three minutes.*

The study confirmed that the way we interact as humans—and as adults with our partners and friends—is rooted in the same impulse: We want to be listened to; we want to be interesting to people who care about us.

The Five A's of Curious Connection

> If you are curious, you'll find the puzzles around you. If you are determined, you will solve them. —ERNO RUBIK

To be curious means that we are not the solo actor in the movie of our lives. It means confidently admitting that we don't know it all, we haven't seen it all, we can still learn and grow from others. It takes guts. But we don't always know how. Or perhaps we have been hurt, and our willingness to be open to others has atrophied some. We may need to jump-start our curiosity.

We are going to make that happen.

First, let's look at the benefits—what I call the "five A's." Curiosity toward others leads to the following:

1. **Availability.** Open your full self to others. Being curious expands our worldviews, enhancing what we already know and believe; this deepening makes us more interested in, and interesting to, others.
2. **Adventure.** Lean into your inquisitive nature. Gathering new experiences with our partners, friends, and loved ones bolsters our relationships with the vital memory building and intimacy we crave.

3. **Appreciation.** Learn something deep and true about someone else. Asking leads to valuing others in new and powerful ways.

4. **Acceptance.** Break down avarice, hardened positions, and bitterness. Or as the old saying goes, "Put the shoe on the other foot." Empathy building has long been researched as a key to an exceptional life. French mathematician, inventor, and theologian Blaise Pascal once said, "To understand is to forgive."

5. **Attraction.** Lock into your whole being by expressing deep interest in someone else. Pay them complete attention by fully listening, your eyes locked with theirs. You're both bound to feel your senses ignited.

Writing Prompt: Work Your Curiosity Muscles

Think of someone in your life that you already know very well. Now, reflect and write five things you're curious about—things that you've never asked them before:

1. _____

2. _____

3. _____

4. _____

5. _____

Now, pick one. And ask them.

Kristina Puts Herself Out There

A time when I was brave?

Stepping onto a dance floor even though I despise dancing, picking myself up from the fetal position on the kitchen
floor after my divorce, setting boundaries with my daughter,
trying anything for the first time, chasing a man out of the
DMV to tell him he was beautiful, breaking old patterns, sitting with myself when I'm in pain, standing in my truth.

Isn't it funny how we do that? Dismiss our bravery, dismiss
our accomplishments, dismiss our dreams?

"Oh, anyone would have done that," we say.

"It's not really that big of a deal," we concede.

"I have a long way to go," we sigh.

I recall a conversation with my neighbor that I had shortly
after a particularly dark period in my life. I was nursing a broken heart (sometimes I feel like a girl with way too many of
them—a mirror maze of them—and they shatter one by one,
and sometimes simultaneously, disorienting and scaring me).
I had recently stopped drinking and was suffering from a general sense of inadequacy, loss, and loneliness. My neighbor listened attentively as I catalogued "all the things."

When I finally stopped rambling long enough for her to get
a word in, she looked at me. That deep-in-the-eyes stare where
you know something important is about to happen. That look
and silence that precedes things like death pronouncements
or first kisses. You aren't sure what is coming, but you know it
is something significant.

"You are so brave," she said.

The words hung there for a moment, hungry to stay, but
then I did what I always do and started distancing myself
from the compliment. "Not really. What choice did I have?

There is a nine-year-old little girl in there depending on me to get it together and go on."

"You know, some people choose not to get it together, not to go on, right?"

Hmm. She's right.

I am still stumbling through life, but I am doing it sober, and more present, and more vulnerable than before. And doing it this way has led to results nothing short of magical.

And that, I can now see, is indeed brave.

Curious Introspection

Who looks outside, dreams; who looks inside, awakes.

—CARL JUNG

I stepped into Rhonda Britten's two-day Fearless Living workshop based on her book of the same name[5] with a bit of a chip already on my shoulder. As you must know by now, I disagree with the notion that any of us could or should truly lead a "fearless" life.

A great writer and speaker, Rhonda shared her very personal story with our group. At the age of fourteen, she witnessed her father murder her mother in a jealous rage and then kill himself. After a twenty-year-long downward spiral of doubt, self-blame, and addiction that followed that tragic event, she began a years-long quest to understand the fear that had engulfed her.

She shared a number of powerful anecdotes, but strangely enough, it was the story about her favorite color that stuck with me the most. To this day, for me, it remains a powerful metaphor for paying deep attention to ourselves.

Here's how it went: During Rhonda's adulthood, someone asked her what her favorite color was. "Green," she answered emphatically. Because, in fact, green had always been her favorite color.

But Rhonda, being the inquisitive type, did something most people don't: She stopped and thought, *But is it really?* She reflected back, racking her brain to remember how she came to confirm that green was the bee's knees. After some time, the answer bubbled into her consciousness. And it was amazing: When Rhonda was in kindergarten, she had a crush on a boy in her class. It turned out that he liked the color green. To court his favor, she told her fellow five-year-olds that her favorite color was green, too. *And then Rhonda didn't question that fact about herself again for decades.*

I sat dumbfounded in our working group. I thought about it. My favorite color—forever, it seemed—had always been brick red. And then, sitting there in that small room in rural Massachusetts with twenty coaches, academics, and mental health professionals, I remembered in a flash how my love of brick red came to be.

It was in kindergarten for me, too. I remember the box of Crayola crayons passed around a circle of students. I was asked to pull out the one that represented my favorite color. Brick red seemed like the best choice in that moment, and so it was. And I never questioned it.

It begs *these* questions: How well do you really know yourself? What assumptions have you made about yourself—or been told by others—and not reassessed in years?

Writing Prompt: Recover What You May Have Buried

My favorite color is _____

_____

My favorite song is _____

_____

My greatest joy in life is _____

_____

A crazy idea I've been harboring is _____

_____

The one thing that I could do today that would be outrageously fun would be _____

_____

My last meal would be _____

_____

The place I would most like to travel to in the world is _____

_____

_____

My favorite guilty pleasure is _____

_____

I wish that _____

_____

I worry that _____

_____

The place where I find my greatest peace is _____.

_____

_____

Scare Your Soul Challenge: Go on a Self-Date

Set a date on your calendar when you commit to going out for a meal on your own. This will be, I promise, a meal that you will always remember.

In addition to being completely alone, don't bring anything to read, and leave your phone at home or in the car. Your goal is to spend this time by yourself, in public.

Yes, you might feel strange. OK, you *will* feel strange. But focus on the experience: Study everything around you. Look at your food and really take time to taste and enjoy it. Get curious about the workings of your own mind: How are you feeling in the moment? What are you struggling with? Are you really enjoying this amazing sense of freedom and pride in doing this challenge?

Take some time to capture how solo dining felt to you and what you can take from this experience into the future.

_____

_____

_____

"To Fall in Love with Anyone, Do This"

> Perhaps the secret of living well is not in having all the answers but in pursuing unanswerable questions in good company. —RACHEL NAOMI REMEN

Arthur Aron has been studying attraction, intimacy, and connection for over fifty years.

A professor of psychology at Stony Brook University, Aron has developed a robust body of research dealing with how intimate relationships are formed. But one study in particular has made the biggest splash; it attempted to answer an intriguing question: Can the intimacy between two strangers actually be fostered in a lab?

In 2015, Mandy Len Catron catapulted Aron and his research team's work into the public consciousness through a *New York Times* essay entitled, "To Fall in Love with Anyone, Do This."[6]

Catron described Aron's process, in which two strangers sat face-to-face, asking and answering a series of thirty-six increasingly intimate questions. The measurable impact was clear, but there was another outcome Aron might not have expected: a number of his research participants—strangers when they first sat down with each other—ended up getting married.

Aron's set of questions was so powerful because—among other benefits—it encouraged deep listening and active curiosity. The questions were prescribed, so the partners didn't need to create their own. They both got to speak, which freed up the innate desire some of us have to formulate our own answers while someone is speaking. And the questions—on topics ranging from family, memories, and desires—were designed to evoke vulnerability within the safe confines of the exercise.

The final part of Aron's process involved another uniquely intimate act: both partners were instructed to stare into each other's eyes without looking away for four minutes.

When we're curious, when we listen, when we truly see each other, and when we bring our vulnerable selves to the table with someone of value to us, we cannot help but create deep connection.

Getting Intimate

Our first date was a train wreck. Well, the first 99 percent of it was.

Jen and I had matched on a dating app. She worked as a real estate agent specializing in selling high-end properties in Fort Lauderdale. And as far as I could tell via text, she seemed incredibly bright and interesting. Intrigued with each other, we agreed to meet at a wine bar the following week.

If only getting there had been so easy! After a series of colossal errors on my part, including getting lost on the way, being unable to find a parking space, and breaking out into a sweat from an eight-block jog from my car, I finally found the bar with a red neon wine bottle in the window. I was twenty-five minutes late.

When Jen slowly slid off her stool at the bar to say hello, I could tell already she wasn't happy. What Jen *was*…was tall. In heels, she was at least six foot one. I had to peer upward to say hello. We spoke at the bar for a time, swapping superficial stories about recent travels and the selections on the wine list. There was no spark of interest, I could tell, from either of us.

About ready to call it a night, I asked her why she split her time between South Florida and our shared hometown of Cleveland.

"I was diagnosed with a brain tumor and wanted to be close to my family while I was getting treatment," she told me warmly. Curious, I asked more, and she let me into her journey: losing her younger sister to a similar brain cancer, the closeness she felt to her family, and her dogged commitment to fighting her disease. I saw a side of her that inspired and touched me deeply. She was kind, honest, and brave. As we said good night, we agreed to stay in touch.

Two weeks later, Scare Your Soul was hosting one of its challenges. I had read about Arthur Aron's thirty-six questions, and I challenged our community to find someone they didn't know well (or at all) and dive into Aron's questions together. I chose to do the challenge twice with two people I didn't know well. After some thought, I texted Jen. She agreed, and one late Sunday afternoon, a bottle of cabernet in hand, she arrived at my front door.

An hour (and that bottle of cabernet) later, we finished the last of the questions. I had never experienced anything quite like it in my life. Some questions had required us to be brutally honest about our lives, others fostered a sense of closeness, and yet others encouraged us to share deeply about our wants and desires. I learned about Jen as a child, about her struggles and triumphs, and I saw Jen's vulnerability and commensurate strength.

Two hours of superficial chatting at a wine bar had given us but a glimpse of each other, but one hour of curious and vulnerable connection had opened us up to each other completely.

We knew two things as she left that night: She had no room for a romantic relationship since her rigorous treatment schedule required so much time and energy. But more importantly, we knew that the experience had bonded us forever. I knew that this tall, wine-loving woman would be my friend forever.

Jen and I stayed in close touch, and I joined her cancer journey with her. And even though she struggled with the back-and-forth of treatments, the biopsies and scans, the wild euphoria of a good progress report from her doctor, and the depression of the disappointments reported by the lab, she always found time to focus on others. To my constant amazement, she continued to focus on *me*.

When one of my extended family members was diagnosed with prostate cancer, Jen conducted extensive research on the latest treatment options, texting me links, research studies, and holistic remedies for him to try. When I was diagnosed with tinnitus and began to slowly lose my hearing, she connected me with naturopaths, nontraditional remedies, and again, more research. She cajoled me to book my doctor's appointments. Her positivity inspired me and made my own journey easier. We would talk about what we learned about each other over the course of those thirty-six questions, diving deep into the well of knowledge we now had about each other.

On my birthday in June 2019, she brought over a bottle of French wine with the vintage of the year I was born. I promised her I would do the same for her. Unfortunately, I would never have that chance.

Jen passed away peacefully at her home in February 2020. Her loving family members—the ones she had mentioned that first night at the wine bar—were at her side. At her memorial service, tearful at this unknowable loss, we toasted—with wineglasses held high—Jen's forty-two years of life.

As I walked out of the memorial service alone, the sun was setting. And I felt Jen's warm presence. I still do, all the time.

Now, when I am confronted with the choice of staying safe, comfortable, and quiet...or risking being courageous, curious, and vulnerable, the choice is simple:

I take the risk.

Scare Your Soul Challenge: Engage in a Scare Your Soul "Courageous Conversation"

It's time to put it all together. Your challenge is to engage with a partner in Scare Your Soul's version of the thirty-six questions.

We call it a "courageous conversation," and we designed it—inspired by Aron—to deeply enhance your connection with someone. It will push you to ask someone to spend time and energy in pursuit of a deeper relationship. It will work your listening skills. It will require you to be vulnerable. And in the end, it will encourage you to be courageously curious about another person.

It will most likely be a scary experience at first, but here are five helpful guidelines:

1. First, boldly ask someone to participate with you. It can be a close confidant, a stranger, or someone in between. But make the ask, and set a time and place with this person. For the purpose of this exercise, I will call that person your "partner."

2. Find a quiet place where you and your partner can talk without interruption, preferably in person. If you must speak on video, make sure you can see and hear each other clearly.

3. Set aside enough time to engage deeply with the process. A lazy Sunday afternoon would be perfect; I would ballpark at least one and a half hours.

4. Lean into your curiosity. Really be present, listening intently to your partner's words and forgoing any reaction or com-

ment you might be tempted to have. Hold their stories in reverence.

5. For a deep experience, you must bring your full self to your responses. Endeavor to be honest and open. Trust the process.

Part One: Getting Started

Sitting face-to-face, ask and answer the following seven questions. Each of you should answer before moving to the next question. Feel free to ask clarifying questions if you wish after your partner finishes each answer.

1. What was the best book you've read in the last six months, and why did you love it?
2. What was the best gift you've ever received, and what about it made it so special?
3. What was your favorite smell growing up, and why?
4. Design your "perfect hour." If you could do anything in the world for sixty minutes, what would you do?
5. Share an embarrassing story that you've rarely (if ever) shared.
6. Finish this sentence: "The thing I am avoiding most in life right now is…"
7. What was one hard time that you've had in life, and what did it teach you?

Part Two: Sharing Desires

1. Describe one emotion that you would want to feel if everything went really well in your life.
2. If you won $10 million in the lottery today, rattle off the things that you would absolutely do tomorrow.
3. What is one thing about your relationship with your conversation partner that you cherish, and why?
4. What is one true talent that you possess that could make the world better in some way?

Take a break and take time to congratulate each other for great work.

Now, onward!

Part Three: Focusing on Growth

1. No matter who we are, we all feel envy at times. That emotion can actually tell us a lot about what we desire in life. So, name one person—living or dead—whom you envy. Explain what about them makes you feel envious.
2. What is one single thing that one of your loved ones could do that would make your life happier?
3. What is one way that you believe you could enhance your own physical, intellectual, or spiritual life that you are not doing now?
4. What is one personal problem that you are going through now?

Set a timer on your phone for four minutes. Sit—again—facing your conversation partner. Without using any words, look into each other's eyes. Open yourselves to each other. Be open to being truly seen.

Part Four: Mutual Commitments

You've reached the final stage. Take time to make a firm commitment to do the following with your partner in the next three months:

- Choose one thing that you will do together that is wild, silly, or crazy. (FYI, karaoke is an absolutely acceptable choice.)
- Do one thing for each other that would make each of you happier. It could be as minor as a neck massage or as large as a hiking trip in Patagonia. You both decide.
- Agree to do one random act of kindness together.

Key Insights

1. Creating our first Scare Your Soul challenge—buying coffee for a stranger and maintaining an openness to curiosity about that person—exemplified how small acts of connection feed our souls.

2. Human connection is a powerful and deeply important part of an exceptional life. The longest longitudinal study on human happiness has found, unequivocally, that deep social connections make us happy and healthy.

3. We are hardwired to be curious, which creates a boost in activity in the hippocampus and releases dopamine. Curiosity lights up our brains in many of the same ways that money, sex, and roller coasters do.

4. Curiosity is a powerful gateway to social connection, allowing us to interact with other people with an open mind and open heart. That sense of curiosity leads to some tangible benefits, which we call the "five A's": availability, adventure, appreciation, acceptance, and attraction.

5. When we bring curiosity and vulnerability together in a "courageous conversation," deep intimacy can be created. Inspired by psychologist Arthur Aron's work, Scare Your Soul developed a process by which two people can engage with each other in a mindset of curiosity and honesty. Amazing things flow from this level of personal engagement.

CHAPTER 12

Courage Principle Five: Awe

Here is my secret, a very simple secret: It is only with the heart
that one can see rightly; what is essential is invisible to the eye.

—ANTOINE DE SAINT-EXUPÉRY

For decades, I've walked a mile-long path that cuts through a local park not far from home. It's both a private and public space, as it's generally secluded from the noise and tumult of traffic, and yet every few minutes a biker or jogger seems to pass by. We meet eyes, and most often we share a brief smile.

I've traveled this stretch of narrow pavement for years, oftentimes when I needed solace or perspective: when the kids were struggling at school, when I was about to get divorced, when a major work decision had to be made, and when a dear friend's cancer returned.

And although I've walked the path at all times of the year, it feels most powerful to me in autumn. I walk through November's bracing air, wet leaves just short of freezing under my shoes, my jacket pulled up tight against my neck. I feel a deep sense of awe at my autumnal surroundings and, in a deeper way, for my life. I feel at once small and vast, individual and interconnected. The experience feels holy.

Awe—just like fear, anger, or joy—has the potential to give us new perspective, meaning, and acceptance. Awe is the intense emotional response we experience when in the presence of an object, event, idea, or person that's extraordinary.

Your Path

I believe that the greatest truths of the universe don't lie outside, in the study of the stars and the planets. They lie deep within us, in the magnificence of our heart, mind, and soul. Until we understand what is within, we can't understand what is without. —ANITA MOORJANI

We all have paths or routes we take where we feel alive, aware, and inspired. Our paths are places we've walked, spaces where we feel at ease, free to think and notice. Steps feel solid and right. Ideas and epiphanies might arise as we traverse these paths. And when we return to life—from our path walks—we feel edified.

Where is *your* path?

Getting Awestruck

The invariable mark of wisdom is to see the miraculous in the common. —RALPH WALDO EMERSON

I recently watched a video on YouTube of a baby cradled in her mother's arms. The baby, deaf and only a few months old, had a hearing aid in her ear and was about to hear her mother's voice for the very first time in her life. As her mom speaks and coos those first words, the baby's face moves through an amazing range of emotions—first, complete confusion, then a trembling lip as if she would cry. Finally, a tentative, small smile creeps to her lips.

Awe isn't simple. It's an emotion that most of us don't just leap into. And yes, it can elicit a range of reactions. Awe seems grand, impressively vast, elusive, a vestige of a bygone era or something that resides in the hushed corner of church.

In terms of its definitive qualities, researchers typically describe awe as having two separate components:

- It has a quality of vastness or transcendence. We feel small in comparison to the experience we are having or what we are seeing, but at the same time we also experience a deep feeling of connectedness.
- It somehow challenges our typical way of perceiving life and encourages us to see the world—and our place in it—in an expanded way. Quite often, awe results in the need to alter existing belief structures—sometimes in profound and life-changing ways—to accommodate the experience and its implications.

For centuries, awe was a scary concept, mostly aligned with feelings of dutiful respect and near dread. In fact, the word itself has its roots in the Old Norse word *agi*, which means "fright."

Over the years, we've developed a better understanding of the term. Ralph Waldo Emerson—never one to be called coy—experienced a fit of awe on a walk through a forest and wrote, "Standing on the bare ground, my head bathed by the blithe air and uplifted into infinite space, all mean egotism vanishes. I become a transparent eyeball."[1]

The humanistic psychologist Abraham Maslow is likely known more for his work in developing his "hierarchy of needs," but he also wrote about "peak experiences" that could be studied, understood, and utilized in order to live a better life. Maslow wrote of such experiences as "joyous and exciting moments in life, involving sudden feelings of intense happiness and wellbeing, wonder and awe."[2]

The emotion begs us to embody Emerson's entrancing concept of a "transparent eyeball": getting out of our own way, appreciating and drinking in our surroundings, and seeing life in a more wondrous light. It begs us to see life as it is, in its infinite connectedness.

It begs us to say "*wow*" way more often than we would otherwise.

Writing Prompt: Getting to "Wow"

English writer, journalist, actor, and sportsman George Plimpton had a passionate fascination—bordering on an all-out love affair—with fireworks. *Yes, fireworks.* It's where he found his sense of awe most profoundly.

He once wrote, "It was the frustration of not being able to put on paper what was so vivid in one's mind...compared with the simple act of igniting a fuse and immediately producing a great chrysanthemum of color and beauty high above, punctuated with a splendid concussion, while, below, people would gape in wonderment and call out 'Wow!'"[3]

I invite you to think back: When was a time you remember feeling wowed?

Maybe it was a fireworks display, your first sporting event or concert, a walk in nature. What happened, and how did it make you feel?

_____

_____

_____

_____

The Power of Awe

> Wonder is the heaviest element on the periodic table. Even a tiny fleck of it stops time. —DIANE ACKERMAN

Psychologists have been studying awe and its effects in lab and field research studies for years. In the field, they've determined that feelings of awe—spawned by viewing beautiful images, hearing inspirational speeches, or being told meaningful stories—create major shifts in consciousness.

In short, they discovered the following:

- Awe optimizes expansive thinking that transcends boundaries, allowing us to be more courageously innovative and creative.
- Awe encourages us toward acts of service and generosity.
- Awe is a gateway to a more spiritual, faithful, or universalist life, where we see value in things that are unseen or unknown.
- Awe opens our eyes to the beauty, grace, and uniqueness of others around us, allowing us to rise above petty judgments and formulations.
- Awe is the fuel for indescribably powerful experiences of art, music, food, sunrises, and more.

Finally, researchers discovered that in overworked, overburdened lives, awe helps bring us into the present. Living "in the moment" encourages peace, reflection, clarity, and memory.

Writing Prompt: How Does Awe Exist in Your Life Now?

In your journal or on a piece of paper, reflect on the following:

1. What blocks you from feeling a sense of awe? Were there past experiences—whether through religion, your upbringing, or comments from parents or grandparents—that stopped you from opening yourself up to an awe experience?
2. When was the last time you saw something "vast"—something so dramatically larger than you that it took your breath away? Describe your emotions and thoughts in that moment.
3. When do you notice that you are most moved to awe? When you hear a beautiful piece of music? Or see an architectural wonder, a painting, a beautifully designed room? Or when you watch the tides shift, witness a stunning sunset, or cradle a newborn baby in your arms?

4. Write about a time when you saw someone else having an awe-inspiring moment. Maybe it was at a museum, a concert, or an aquarium. Maybe it was a child experiencing something for the very first time. What did it bring up for you?

5. Take note: The fact that you are alive, safe, and breathing is one of the rarest feats of survival. Generations of your ancestors had to survive, meet, and mate to make your very existence possible. You are a miracle. Feel more self-love and kindness with this realization. Write about how "awe-some" it is that you exist.

Christa Listens to the Answer

I was twenty-eight years old and had everything I'd ever wanted in life: a beautiful but modest home, two dogs, an Ivy League master's degree, an acclaimed art career, and a job as an assistant professor of photography at a prestigious college in New England.

I'd fought hard for that life, beating the odds. My mother was a career waitress. She raised my beloved identical twin sister, Cara, and me on her own with that low wage. Mom grew up in a nine-hundred-square-foot, two-bedroom house in Albany, New York, the youngest of five children to good Catholic, first-generation Italian-American parents. Mom's father was a housepainter. Her mother was a house cook. Mom's grandparents were fruit farmers: nothing was ever squandered or risked. In short, people in my family didn't go to college, let alone stand at the front of the room teaching at one.

Cara was a writer. A truly talented writer. And ever since I was a little girl, I'd wanted to be a writer, too. But twins are competitive. And because of that, and because I'd loved her so, I went on happily to my art career. End of story. Or so I thought.

And then, the summer we turned twenty-nine, Cara died of a heroin overdose, a death of despair. That loss was like having my soul ripped out. Or being asked to live in a body without bones. Or—because we looked exactly alike—as if I'd died, too: Looking at myself in the mirror, I was looking at Cara. Going to and planning Cara's funeral was like planning and attending my own funeral.

Time passed on my grief. Little by little, the life shock of losing my twin emboldened me to reassess my life. I asked myself, *Am I happy at my job? Do I really want to live in New England? If I could pick again, what would my life look like?* It was equal parts terrifying and exhilarating. Practicality dogged me. I had no safety net. No real money. And the little voice in my head told me that thirty was too old to start over. But instead of yielding to worry, I saved every penny I earned and made the bold choice to apply to a master's program in creative writing.

And here I am now, fifteen years after losing my twin sister. I've published two best-selling books, won fellowships for writing, and I'm a professor of creative writing at a prestigious graduate school. I have three young children. Two beautiful dogs. And a house in Pittsburgh. I wouldn't have the life I have now if I hadn't lost Cara. But I did lose her. And I can't change that.

The lesson I've taken from this journey is that we must pay attention to what we want and need. And then listen to the answer.

Because even when you're an identical twin, you only live once.

Finding Awe in Daily Life

There are only two ways to live your life. One is as though nothing is a miracle. The other is as though everything is a miracle.

—ALBERT EINSTEIN

We don't have to travel to the Himalayas or sit below the glow of the northern lights to experience a sense of awe. It's readily accessible and only requires the courage to open our minds—and even more so our hearts—to it.

But how do we get there? First, acknowledge that despite how it may feel, your life is not routine. Why not choose to see it that way, acknowledging every moment as uniquely extraordinary and potentially awe-filled?

And then, why not *lead* life that way? Getting stuck in your comfort zone can result in a life that feels routine and uninspired; awe can pierce through the monotony.

Awe—an emotion we have access to at all times—illuminates the power, vastness, connection, and transcendence of our lives.

Get small to get big. Be amazed by your life. Open your eyes and ears to nature, people, and experiences. See the interconnections between you and your world. Look at yourself in the mirror with reverence.

You may ask, "This sounds simple, so why does awe take courage?"

In order to access awe, we have to embrace that we're not the center of the universe. Experiencing awe means loosening our sense of control to accommodate the unknowable. It relies more on faith than fact (which is harder for some of us than others). It changes our relationship with time and connects us with others who we may feel are not like us. Awe crosses boundaries between people and ideologies—it forces us to see others as fellow members of the human race.

Every bit of this requires courage.

Writing Prompt: Finding Your Awe

Name one thing in your life that awes you. Describe what it is and how it makes you feel in that moment of wonder. Really dig deep and express your feelings.

_____

_____

_____

Hacking Awe with Sliding Door Moments

> It is easy to see the branches of trees moving, but it takes
> practice to see the wind. —ELAINE SMITH GENSER

Are you open to the concept that there is something greater than you at work in your life? Does that feel scary? I'm not talking specifically about God—although you may very well choose to cherish belief in a higher power—but rather the idea that you and I don't have it all figured out. Maybe we don't completely hold the reins in this rodeo.

Maybe things actually do happen for a reason. And maybe we can hold a feeling of awe in it all if we choose to see it that way.

When we practice holding a sense of wonder and gratitude—a key concept we addressed earlier in the book—we begin to see our lives suffused with meaning. This practice is particularly evident when we consider "sliding door moments." Dr. John Gottman (and later, Brené Brown in her book _Daring Greatly_) named these after the 1998 movie starring Gwyneth Paltrow. If you are unfamiliar with the film, Paltrow portrays Helen, a London public relations executive unceremoniously "sacked" from her high-powered job. As she races to catch a train to get home, the arc of her story splits into two; in one scenario, she barely makes the train. In the other, the door closes before she can make it. For the balance of the movie, we see the implications of this one bifurcating moment: two completely different lives separated by the simple act of making—or missing—a train.

Cultivating a sense of awe for the sliding door moments in our journey is one way to "hack" a sense of awe.

How?

Think of this: Can you feel a sense of awe in recognizing, with just a single turn left instead of right, a phone call made instead of not, or a word spoken instead of silenced, that the life you are living could have been drastically different? It's both jarring and inspiring to see how tenuous (and seemingly insignificant) small acts or decisions have on our futures.

So, let me now ask you to be courageous. I want you to find awe. I want you to find and revel in a sliding door moment in your life.

You ready?

Scare Your Soul Challenge: Feel Awe in Your Own Sliding Door Moment

Pick one person in your life that you've met in the last ten years who is dear to you. They're not a relative; they're somebody you've met outside of your family unit.

Write their name. Now, write one sentence about what they mean to you.

_____

_____

Think back to the moment when you met.

What was the date? What time of day was it? Where were you? What else was happening in your life at the time?

_____

_____

Now, finally, think back on the things that happened that day that actually got you to the moment of meeting that person.

Write down five things that potentially could have delayed you or redirected you that day.

For example, *I could have missed the bus that got me to that meeting.* Or, *I usually don't go to restaurants on Tuesday nights.* Or, *If my car hadn't just been fixed the day before, I wouldn't have been able to drive there.* Or, *My babysitter could have canceled.*

1. _____
2. _____
3. _____
4. _____
5. _____

But those things didn't stop you. You did make it. And you met someone who changed you and who made your life better. And now, you probably can't even imagine life without this person, right? Feel the awe in this realization. Wrangle through the things that had to conspire to make this union possible.

Now, hold that feeling in your heart. Call or email that person and let them know what they mean to you.

Simone Takes a Giant Leap of Faith

In South Africa in the early '70s, my grandmother's friend Robbie would take me swimming at the public pool. I loved spending time in her apartment overlooking the Atlantic Ocean, because I knew no one else who lived like her.

Robbie taught me many things. She taught me how to stretch my body, about her beloved Switzerland, about healthy food, and the value of caring for one's body. Robbie was also mentoring my mother about yoga and vegetarianism. My parents adopted this lifestyle, and those teachings became a part of me.

Some forty years later, I was living in Ohio in an unhappy marriage and dreading the long winters. Longing for a change in scenery, I rented a tiny cottage in Ojai, California, for a month. I enrolled the kids in a summer camp at a local school founded by the Indian philosopher Krishnamurti (whom I had never heard of). I was enthralled with the campus, with its rustic oak tree grove and views of the Ojai Valley. I remember thinking that it would be an absolute dream for the kids to attend school there, and the impossibility of that ever happening.

A year later, with compromise and sacrifice, and the support of my co-parent, the kids and I moved across the country. There was no rational reason for this move. Just a giant leap of faith.

The kids had been at school for six months when my mom came to visit. When she noticed a picture of Krishnamurti hanging at the school, she asked if I remembered Robbie. She explained that Robbie had been a devout follower of Krishnamurti, visiting Switzerland each year and learning about yoga and vegetarianism. I had never connected the dots. In an instant, a circle closed across space and time.

Of course it made perfect sense that we were living in Ojai, and the kids were enrolled in Krishnamurti's school. Our life may not have seemed to make practical sense to others, but to me it felt perfectly right.

Living Life in Radical Amazement

Grandeur or mystery is something with which we are confronted everywhere and at all times.

—ABRAHAM JOSHUA HESCHEL

For many of us, the Covid pandemic stole some of our simplest joys. The hugs we could give a loved one, seeing a jazz band live, sitting inside a cozy restaurant, greeting a co-worker first thing in the morning. All gone. And with that, a deep sense that maybe we took some of those things for granted. That maybe we could have felt a sense of awe or reverence in what seemed like the most minor of things.

The concept of awe was on my mind as I stood in front of a room of fifty nonprofit professionals in Miami. I could feel their concern for my mental stability, mainly because I had just personally given each one of them the key to a lesson on awe's first cousin, a powerful practice that author and theologian Abraham Joshua Heschel called "radical amazement."

I had just handed each one of them a raisin.

So, if you are open to trying out this experience, procure a raisin if you can. Pick up a pack from your local bodega, swipe one from your kid's lunch box—whatever it takes. If not, use your amazing powers of imagination. You now have a raisin in your hand. Contemplate it briefly. Nothing much to think about.

It's a raisin, after all.

Now, open your mind just a bit and consider the following:

- Imagine your raisin's birth as a fledgling grape on its vine. Where was it—California, Greece, Turkey? And what is its lineage? Could it be a Black Corinth, Thompson Seedless, Fiesta, or Muscat?
- Think of all of the rain and the sunshine that was lavished on your raisin as it grew.
- Think of the ancient farming and drying process that resulted in this raisin. The process started with the Egyptians four thousand years ago and was handed down from generation to generation. Even with technological advances, many of the same traditions exist today.
- Think of the people involved in getting the raisin to you. The ones who planted the vines, pruned them, harvested the

grapes on a late August day, dried them, packed them. Think of the truckers who got them across the country, those that unpacked them and placed them on the shelves, the checkout person who smiled at you as they handed you your receipt.

- Think of its powerfully small organic package—less than 15 percent of its original moisture content remains—full of vitamins, minerals, iron, copper, and zinc. It has a low pH, naturally resists spoiling, and has a sweetness provided completely by nature.
- Look at the exterior—the wrinkles and crevices. How they absorb or reflect light. Each like a fractal or a snowflake, forever unique.
- Pop it in your mouth. First, let it sit on your tongue; feel the flavor unfolding slowly. The taste developing as the enzymes in your saliva interact with the chemical compounds. How it softens. How it becomes an experience rather than an afterthought.

How does the concept of a simple raisin feel now? The same? Different?

When we take the time to think, reflect, understand, honor, and sanctify, even the lowly can actually feel exalted. Our experience has entered the realm of amazement. Heschel once wrote, "Our goal should be to live life in radical amazement...get up in the morning and look at the world in a way that takes nothing for granted."[4]

It takes courage to live this way. Why?

Because we are attuned to be immediately entertained and amused. We are attuned to the concrete, the clear, the controllable. Amazement requires a leap of faith. It requires time, effort, and consideration. It requires an engagement with the world.

Think of the power of leading a life where even the smallest details can become items of wonder and where your daily experience helps to inspire and teach others around you to do the same.

This is power beyond power. Even the lowly raisin proves it.

Writing Prompt: Being Radically Amazed

What is one simple thing in your life that you currently take for granted? Take a step back and go through the process illuminated with the raisin we just discussed. How can you view it in an exalted, awestruck kind of way? Write down your experience and how your thinking might now change.

Key Insights

1. Awe was originally viewed as an emotion full of dread; more recently, psychologists and researchers have found that awe is a positive emotion that can be accessed by any of us at any time. Awe is typically understood as a sense of vastness coupled with an act of accommodation, an expansion, or a change in our belief system.

2. Awe has powerful and positive effects on our lives, making us happier, healthier, more giving, less stressed, and more grateful. These are all avenues that will also lead to a more fulfilled Scare Your Soul life.

3. The possibility of awe is all around us, and not just in places of worship or forests. When we are courageous enough to open our eyes and hearts to the wonder of our daily lives, we flourish.

4. Sliding door moments are one way of "hacking" a sense of awe; they allow us to recognize that we are living a life that—in a heartbeat—could have taken a drastically divergent path.

5. The process of radical amazement—a component of awe—
   is the powerful experience of seeing the exalted and transcendent in even the smallest things. Waking up in the
   morning, our coffee, the people we love, sunshine, cool dew
   on the grass, watching a football game with a loved one—all
   moments ripe for appreciation and awe.

CHAPTER 13

Courage Principle Six: Forgiveness

Forgiveness is not weak. It takes courage to face and overcome powerful emotions. —DESMOND TUTU

The truth tore a hole in my heart when I opened the box of love letters she had mistakenly stacked on her nightstand.

We'd been dating for nearly two years, and my love for her had no beginning or end. She was a Wisconsin-born wild child—long hair, ripped jeans, taking huge bites from life, mixing laughter and tears in the very same sentence. It was my first serious relationship.

One summer Saturday afternoon, we checked the listings in the wrinkled newspaper that sat on a coffee shop table, and decided to check out the Cosmo, a new club, that night.

The Cosmo was absolutely buzzing. After an hour on the dance floor, we sat at the bar together, sweaty and smiling. As I leaned in toward the bartender to order two drinks, I noticed a handsome guy a few seats down glance her way. The glance lingered for a moment, enough for me to take note.

A while later, as I walked alone through the throbbing music toward the club's bathroom, I remember feeling flush with pride that I, indeed, was dating the most amazing woman in the world. Later, she and I walked out into the breeze, arm in arm.

Several months later, as she was putting on makeup in her

bathroom, I noticed the letters, standing upright like soldiers in a box with its lid half-off. Assuming they were mine, I reached in.

The handwriting on the envelope was different. I opened it. It was a love letter written by the handsome guy who had been sitting several seats down at the bar. She had been dating him secretly from that night on.

Pianist George Winston's plaintive album *December* was playing in the background. At that moment, it became the soundtrack for the depression that would engulf me.

Taking Our Power Back

> He who is devoid of the power to forgive is devoid of the power to love. —REVEREND MARTIN LUTHER KING JR.

How have *you* changed when you experienced a trauma?

Being cheated on by someone I loved so deeply forced me backward. I constructed an emotional wall so high that no romantic partner—for years to come—could scale it.

The process went like this: I entered romantic relationships with an open heart and mind, but as soon as my girlfriend and I would get really close, I would instinctually pull back. I would withhold just enough attention so my girlfriend would throw in the towel and call it quits. I would build an elaborate story around my actions, and that became my narrative. "I just want to date," I told people. "I've got plans," I would say. "I can't get too serious."

But the truth was, I was scared to death of being hurt. Relationship after relationship sailed in on a strong breeze only to go down like a shipwreck. Now I bring that awareness in my work to help others.

In my role as a coach for divorcing men, I've heard all of the stories and I've seen all of the pain.

I've borne witness to dreams of marriages and families—of shared futures mused about on honeyed afternoons—being laid to rest. I've seen the page inevitably turning, and for many, the transitions commence: husbands becoming single fathers; homes becoming apartments; dear friendships becoming memories; loud fights becoming silence.

And yet, in the moments when everything solid seems to be shifting below their feet, something grows: the small seed of a new life.

It's a singular life now, but where to plant that seed is their choice. And each day that follows offers a litany of choices: how to co-parent, to spend scarce resources, to manage schedules, to somehow be in two places at once when games and recitals are both scheduled at the same time across town from each other.

Sometimes marriages end on equal footing; oftentimes they don't. Some of the men I've worked with absolutely create the fracture; others are the unwitting recipient. For those men stunned into a cycle of pain, there is one practice—one singular act—that's the key to their entrance into a new life. Truthfully, it evades many of them. They cannot muster its requirements. But the few that have the courage reap rewards: connection, humility, love, self-efficacy, and yes, freedom.

That act is the practice of radical forgiveness.

Of course, this practice is exclusive to neither men nor divorce. It's a practice seated at the heart of most major religions. Forgiveness has been written about as a human virtue for millennia and is scientifically proven to contribute to a full-throated, flourishing life.

And yet, it is so damn hard to actually do.

As we begin the exploration of forgiveness as a means toward a transformational, Scare Your Soul life, I have four concepts I'd ask you to consider:

1. *Some people we love will cause us great pain.*
2. *Their actions will move us to construct high walls built of resentment, disgust, anger, and bitterness to serve as protection from re-experiencing that hurt.*

3. *We can absolutely live quite comfortably behind those walls, residing in the toxicity of a story that ties us to our past. It works, but at a cost.*

4. *Alternatively, we can choose to courageously forgive those who've wronged or damaged us, reclaiming the emotional real estate they occupy. We can fill that property with dignity, confidence, and joy.*

Are you ready to dig deep and go step-by-step into what it means to forgive in your own life?

Let's start with a warm-up exercise.

Writing Prompt: When We Practice Forgiveness Every Single Day

I invite you to consider this: Do you already forgive the petty and annoying miscues of family, friends, and co-workers? What about your uncle's slightly off-color jokes, your sibling who is always late, or the guy who cut in front of you at a busy intersection? These occurrences rank low in emotional magnitude, and we shrug them off. Sometimes we laugh them off. And yes, we forgive their affront.

Try this: list five recent instances when you forgave a small offense:

1. _____

2. _____

3. _____

4. _____

5. _____

Now that you know you've got the muscles, let's dive deeper.

Forgiveness and Fear

> Not forgiving is like drinking rat poison and then waiting
> for the rat to die. —ANNE LAMOTT

Dr. Fred Luskin, head of Stanford University's Forgiveness Project, defines forgiveness as the "peace and understanding that comes from lessening the blame of that which has hurt you, taking your life experience less personally, and seeing the cost of holding a grudge."[1] Dr. Robert Enright, co-founder of the International Forgiveness Institute, puts it even more simply, defining it as "choosing to be good to those who are not good to us."[2]

And there are real health benefits to the practice. The Mayo Clinic reports that letting go of grudges and bitterness can lead to:

- Healthier relationships
- Improved mental health
- Less anxiety, stress, and hostility
- Lower blood pressure
- Fewer symptoms of depression
- A stronger immune system
- Improved heart health
- Improved self-esteem[3]

So, if forgiveness is so good for us, why is it so hard to practice?

As Dr. Luskin has articulated in multiple talks and interviews, the process is so challenging, in part, because our brains crave habits, and negative habits are intrinsically easier to create than the positive ones. Habitually leaning into anger, disgust, and bitterness is easier than leaning into appreciation, kindness, and humility. In addition, holding grudges feeds superficial goodies to our egos, which are insatiably hungry for any reason to hold on to bitterness.

Energy: Hurt, anger, and resentment bolster emotional energy. We experience these feelings and feel a rush sparked with purpose. This chain of feeling provides a focus for combatting disappointments, betrayals, disparity, and trauma. Think about the sensation generated while watching the final runner for your country's Olympic team drop the baton during the gold-medal round; you yell at your TV screen, your frustration palpable, automatic. It's negative, yes, but feels so powerful in the moment.

Clarity: We crave a sense of clarity while lost in betrayal's fog. When we are confused and in pain and desperate to make sense of it all, we solidify blame. We search for a common enemy, a sense of moral superiority and certitude, and a bad guy as foil to us as hero or heroine in our own story.

Community: How many times has someone called you and said, "You won't believe what _____ did to me!"? When we are hurt, we rally our community around us, telling the story (as we see it) to curry support for our ongoing emotional crusade.

Here is the reality: Many of the things others have done to us seem "unforgivable." Abuse, disregard, acts that cost lives or livelihoods—all of these can be so painful that some of us may never feel safe to forgive. The path of radical forgiveness leads not to accepting bad actions but to freeing ourselves from the mental tyranny that those actions caused. This, dear reader, is not mild work; this is hard, gritty, sometimes uncomfortable work.

In his book *Calm Surrender,* Kent Nerburn writes,

> Forgiveness cannot be a disengaged, pastel emotion. It is demanded in the bloodiest of human circumstances, and it must stand against the strongest winds of human rage and hate. To be a real virtue, engaged with the world around us, it must be muscular, alive, and able to withstand the outrages and inequities of inhuman and inhumane acts. It must be able to face the dark side of the human condition.[4]

This work tests our fears. Just remember:

1. Forgiving someone does not mean that the hurtful act is acceptable. We can choose to forgive the actor without condoning the action.
2. The offending party can be part of the process, or not. They may be willing and able, and they may not. They may not be living anymore. That is irrelevant to the process.
3. This practice is done with a full heart, with courage, and without the necessity of a response. The act is the outcome.
4. Forgiving is not about forgetting, bargaining, approving, justifying, or ceasing emotion; it is about taking courageous steps toward winning freedom over past hurts.

Going Deep with the Practice

> As I walked out the door toward the gate that would lead
> to my freedom, I knew if I didn't leave my bitterness and
> hatred behind, I'd still be in prison. —NELSON MANDELA

In the depths of the 2020 Covid-19 pandemic, I felt as lost as everyone else around me. Everything that represented stability—my family, friendships, workplace, income, health—seemed to fall into chaos. After stay-at-home orders were lifted but people were still sequestered—churches, synagogues, and mosques still shuttered, gyms and pools empty, concerts and exhibitions canceled—I felt like I had to do something.

I reached out to a friend, Tami, who owns a wonderful yoga studio in my town. I asked if I could offer donation-only meditation sessions once a week via Zoom from her studio. Proceeds from donations would go to benefit frontline workers. She agreed immediately, and for the weeks following, through the darkest days of the pandemic, I led meditations for dozens of fatigued, stressed-out, scared, and completely wonderful people.

One of the meditations I chose to lead those weeks—in addition to those focused exclusively on courage—was one that I felt was perfect for times when we need to dig deep and show love. It's called "metta."

Metta means "loving-kindness" in the Middle Indic dialect of Pali. In the practice, after a centering phase, one repeats a series of phrases. They are simple and meant to evoke a sense of kindness flowing right from the heart. First, one directs the phrases to oneself, then to someone whom we love or admire, then to a neutral person (think of the barista who hands you your coffee or the-sarcastic checkout guy at the grocery store).

The next person we call to mind, and the toughest for me, is someone we don't like or have a toxic or damaged relationship with. Someone who hurt us. With the same open heart, we offer them goodwill.

Meditation teacher and author Sharon Salzberg says, "Practicing metta illuminates our inner integrity because it relieves us of the need to deny different aspects of ourselves. We can open to everything with the healing force of love."[5]

I can tell you this: Words spoken from the heart can melt ice—even for those we have the most avarice toward. Words do indeed heal.

Let's try it:

Find a comfortable position in which to sit. Tune in to your body and sit in a way that feels comfortable but alert.

Allow yourself to feel your breath. Find the place where it feels strongest for you. It may be in the stomach or abdomen. It may be in the chest. Maybe it's at the nostrils, where you can feel a slight cooling as the air comes in and a subtle warmth as you exhale.

When your mind wanders, treat it as an opportunity rather than a problem. Redirect without self-judgment, and kindly return your focus to your breath.

Now, begin by silently offering yourself the following phrases of kindness:

May I be healthy.
May I be happy.
May I be safe.
May I live with ease.

Now, bring to mind a good friend, mentor, or teacher. Picture them in your mind's eye as you offer them the following:

May you be healthy.
May you be happy.
May you be safe.
May you live with ease.

You can let this person go from your mind and bring to mind a neutral person. This is someone you see maybe regularly but don't know very well. It may be a co-worker or a neighbor. Offer this person the same phrases of loving-kindness, connecting with the intention to care about their well-being.

May you be healthy.
May you be happy.
May you be safe.
May you live with ease.

And as you let this neutral person go, you can bring to mind somebody whom you find difficult. Maybe this is someone who hurt you, whom you hold a grudge against. Can you find it in your heart to wish them well? With as much intention as you can, offer them the following from your heart:

May you be healthy.
May you be happy.
May you be safe.
May you live with ease.

Slowly return to your breath. Focus on it, feeling at the same time a sense of pride that you could share such positive, loving wishes for yourself, for a friend, a neutral person, and, so importantly, someone who has caused you pain.

When you feel ready, take one final deep breath.

How do you feel? Can you notice even a tiny energetic shift inside of you from raw emotion toward someone to a greater sense of grace or understanding?

Let's put that sense of understanding into practice with a challenge.

Scare Your Soul Challenge: The Completion Talk

This challenge is inspired by Tuulia Syvänen, a master trainer at the Radical Honesty Institute, an organization that teaches people how to hold tough conversations that lead to stronger relationships. Picture this scenario:

You are navigating your cart through the produce section of your local grocery store, and out of the corner of your eye, you see someone you know. Instead of wanting to engage with them, your response is to steer your cart away and pretend you didn't see them.

Now, try this test:

Who in your life right now would you want to avoid in the produce section because of a disagreement? About whom do you feel queasiness or tightness in your stomach or chest when you think of them? You may have many, but list just one for now:

I would want to avoid _____

Now, dig into your feelings about this person: Why do you have this reaction about them? What happened in the past, what about your relationship is incomplete, and why do you feel uncomfortable?

_____

_____

_____

Now, recognize in this moment that your unresolved issues with this person are in some way holding you back. They are hampering your ability to live fully, even in a small way. When you have a quiet moment, visualize meeting with this person and saying everything that is on your mind. Imagine being really honest and telling them that you feel sad and angry, that there feels like there's something unresolved between you. In your mind, role-play. What do you think they might say? What might be the outcome? This may feel odd for a bit, but stick with it.

Now, I invite you to write about your visualization experience.

_____

_____

_____

Honoring the Dark Times

> Look at how a single candle can both defy and define the darkness. —ANNE FRANK

It may seem counterintuitive, but in order to fully embrace forgiveness, it's helpful to revisit the times when we were really hurt. Because dark times are our teachers. They are the cudgel that helps cut away the excess in our lives, revealing pure awareness. As much as we might wish these moments away, we gain perspective in times of pain and distress. Living in a maelstrom of pain is akin to having one of our senses removed, the others amplified in its absence; our ability to see what is important in life and to be grateful (even in grief or trauma) gets supersized by our taste of it.

And if you question the old adage "You can't see the light without the darkness," just think about how a cold glass of water tastes when you're running in a heat wave. Or how you clutch your child tightly once you find them after they've been lost in a crowd. Or how, after your doctor calls to tell you that your MRI scan is clean, your very being feels so light that it could be a hot-air balloon.

We must honor pain in order to be free from it.

Scare Your Soul Challenge: Asking for Forgiveness

This challenge is critical to your ability to understand how the process feels from both sides. It's your time to place a call asking for forgiveness.

Select someone in your life to whom you owe an apology—someone you've been avoiding or pretending you did nothing wrong to. Now is your opportunity to right that wrong. Very simply, if it feels safe to do so, contact that person and offer a direct, heartfelt apology. Your goal is not one of outcome; your goal is to acknowledge your action and to apologize.

Spend some time thinking about the event that happened, how you made this mistake, and how you plan to apologize. Then breathe, and pick up the phone.

Write about what happened in your apology call. How did you feel asking? What was the response?

_____

_____

_____

Brett's Vulnerability Invites Connection

I stood backstage, terrified.

I had never spoken to an audience of 120 people, let alone 1,200. But the Columbus Chamber of Commerce asked me to keynote its annual event. And something in me knew that sharing my truth, especially one that nobody expected, might help my healing—and the healing of others, too.

I agonized over the speech. I hired people to help. I wrote and rewrote. I got frustrated. I almost quit. I walked onto the stage. Lights. Applause. Then into the deep end I dove.

"I've spent a lot of time in therapy."

The suited-up crowd went silent.

I talked about my abuse. About how my gifts of sensitivity, creativity, and emotion were punished as flaws. About the bravery of my mother. About how I acted out with drugs and alcohol. About the trauma. About the healing.

I shared my belief that it's all been part of a perfect plan. Perfect for what it is and what it is not.

I told them it took me years to untangle old wiring and figure out who I was born to be but that once I did, the whole world opened. I told them that they were the ones we needed.

"This community needs you. Your business needs you. Your family needs you," I finished. "And most importantly, you need you."

People—all 1,200, it seemed—rose to their feet and clapped. Euphoria.

Before I made it back to my car, my phone started blowing up. Emails. Texts. Phone calls. Tweets. DMs. Later, letters came to the office. To my home.

These were not messages of congratulations. They were much more profound.

"Me too."

"I've never told anyone, but…"

"Can you help me?"

"Can we talk?"

"Thank you."

Turns out I'm not the only one with a messy past. Even in a room full of power players. But having the guts to share my messy past has opened new doors, including some inside myself.

Now, there's more speaking. More writing. A podcast. And above all, a fire ignited to see people, to hear people, and to help people.

Five Steps to Radical Forgiveness

For me, forgiveness and compassion are always linked: how do we hold people accountable for wrongdoing and yet at the same time remain in touch with their humanity enough to believe in their capacity to be transformed? —BELL HOOKS

In Scare Your Soul, radical forgiveness falls into five distinct steps, each of which can come at the time of your choosing. You own this process; it shouldn't be rushed. Here's the progression:

Step one: *Find the hurt.*
Step two: *Get present and practice loving-kindness.*
Step three: *Focus on the person, not the act.*
Step four: *Assess your decision whether to forgive.*
Step five: *Actively offer forgiveness from your heart.*

Step One: Find the Hurt

Now that you're ready, reflect again but this time more deeply on the point where hurt exists. Take yourself back to a time when you were hurt by the actions of someone else. What happened, and how did it feel? What sensations do you notice in your body now when you revisit that time?

_____

_____

_____

Step Two: Get Present and Practice Loving-Kindness

Delve into the metta meditation once again. When you find yourself in the phase of the meditation where you offer loving-kindness to someone difficult, choose the person who created the pain in step one. Take the time to really offer them—in your own heart—well wishes if you can.

Step Three: Focus on the Person, Not the Act

Now, bring the offending person to mind.

Reflect upon the following:

Have the grace to understand that they are a wounded person raised by other wounded people. This is not an excuse to accept their behavior but rather an acknowledgment that each one of us carries with us the legacy of those who raised us, people who may have themselves been hurt deeply by others.

Name one trait that you believe you received from your parents or guardians that hasn't served you or that you wish you could change.

_____

_____

_____

Open your mind up to acknowledging that there may be an alternate explanation to what happened other than the understanding that exists in your own head. Certainty is an illusion.

We all view events from our perspective, and while certain facts may be indisputable, they may not tell the whole story.

Write a scenario from the other side. Try to take the other person's view.

_____

_____

_____

Remember your own failings. Understand that you, too, have made mistakes, hurt other people (sometimes intentionally and sometimes not), or otherwise done things you are not proud of. In that recognition, we can find some peace.

Think of a time when you made a mistake that hurt someone else. Bring yourself back to that time and dig deep into the details. As hard as it is, remember it all. Describe here what you did and why you think you did it.

_____

_____

_____

Step Four: Assess Your Decision Whether to Forgive

Take the opportunity to deliberate about whether you truly wish to forgive this person. Consider how it may grant you a sense of dignity, humility, and freedom, and how it may help loved ones who are affected by any bitterness and anger you hold. Because forgiveness is a choice, you can decide not to forgive. You can hold on to the grudge, or you can choose to forgive.

Step Five: Actively Offer Forgiveness from Your Heart

If you chose forgiveness, this is your time. Each transgression, each situation, each relationship is different, and you must be the arbiter for how you choose to express your forgiveness.

You can meet with the offending person face-to-face to talk through what happened and offer forgiveness. Or you can talk over the phone or send an email, expressing in your own words how you feel. Whatever you choose, the important thing is that you focus on your courageous act, not the reaction you may or may not get.

Finally, you may choose not to communicate your forgiveness at all. The other person may not be alive anymore. Or you may not want contact at this time. If this is the case, find a quiet spot, engage in the work we just discussed, and smile.

And wish them well.

An Offering to a Ghost

> Forgiveness is the final form of love.
>
> —REINHOLD NIEBUHR

I finally forgave my first girlfriend. The one with the box of letters.

I tried to find her but couldn't. I tried Facebook, Google; I searched her old home address for clues. Nothing. I don't know if she is living off-the-grid, changed her name, relocated somewhere high in the mountains. But I tried.

And in the end, it really didn't matter.

I found an old photo of her and me, shiny in the bottom of an old box in my basement. She, in a pink satin dress, is smiling. I'm smiling, too. And just looking at that photo made me smile all over again.

Then I sent her a wish from the deepest place within me:

May you be healthy.
May you be happy.
May you be safe.
May you live with ease.

And I felt the burden lift.

Key Insights

1. The ability to forgive, while taking significant courage, can bring us connection, humility, self-efficacy, and a deep sense of freedom from the pain of past hurts.

2. The reality that we will experience pain and trauma in our lives is almost a certainty. The question is this: Will we choose to discharge some of that emotional energy? We can build emotional walls that are meant to keep us safe from future pain, but numbing and protecting don't lead to a flourishing life. Taking risks, opening our hearts, and forgiving when the time is right do.

3. We all practice forgiveness every single day and may not even realize it. We are constantly presented with moments in which we accept the failings and miscues of others (and ourselves).

4. Forgiveness is a concept at the root of many of the world's religions and one that has been practiced as a virtue throughout the millennia. More recent research has found that it has significant health benefits.

5. Forgiveness is challenging for many reasons, not the least of which is the impact that holding grudges has on us. Grudges create energy, give us a sense of clarity (right and wrong) at a time when we feel chaotic emotions, and encourage us to rally support in our cause against the offending party.

6. "Radical forgiveness" does not require that we forgive or condone the offending act itself, or ever require another person to be present in our process. It is about courageously taking our power back. There is a sequential process that includes (1) finding the hurt, (2) getting present and practicing loving-kindness, (3) focusing on the person and not the act, (4) assessing the decision of whether to forgive, and (5) actively offering forgiveness.

CHAPTER 14

Courage Principle Seven: Work

The highest reward for a person's toil is not what they get for it, but what they become by it. —JOHN RUSKIN

My aunt Gail's house glowed like a lantern in the dark.

It was a cold November night. Fresh snow fell and settled on the tops of the four wine bottles as I carried them to the front door. I knew that, inside, my extended family and other assorted guests would be marveling over the turkey, stuffing, cranberry sauce, and Cousin Susan's famous mashed potatoes.

I walked into the dining room and placed the cabernet and chardonnay on the table, surveying the much-loved company. Thanksgiving is an important holiday in my family; more than any other, it's the destination point for relatives of all geographies to come together, update each other, raise toasts. It is our beloved annual opportunity to honor each other and to honor the passage of time. Thanksgiving is that mile marker where we watch our older generation walking inevitably slower as our toddlers transform into teens.

As I scanned Aunt Gail's dining room, I noticed someone I'd never met.

Ron sat in a wheelchair in the middle of the room. He wore khakis and a blue V-neck sweater, his thin gray hair parted over to the side. I watched as the hubbub of children and hot, steaming dishes passed around him. Seeing he was alone, I walked over and introduced myself. He told me in a volume just beyond a whisper that he was a longtime friend of my aunt's and was excited to have been invited—with his wife, Sally—to this event. Most of their own kids, he told me, had moved away a very long time ago.

After some pleasantries, I asked Ron to tell me a bit about his life. He was ninety-four, he told me, his blue eyes attentive to my reaction. He was, he told me, a baseball player when he was young. A really good one. A phenom.

By the age of seventeen—in 1944—Ron was pitching a blistering 101-mile-an-hour fastball. The ball leaving Ron's left hand and arriving at home plate took a mere quarter of a second slower than the blink of a human eye. He struck out opposing batters with abandon.

But his baseball abilities didn't end at being just a player: Ron was a lover and a student of the game, and with deep analysis and after tinkering with his delivery from the mound, he seemed to have figured out something no one else had.

It is generally believed that the reason a pitcher has an edge in the battle against a hitter is that the hitter must contend with two separate forces: speed (how fast the ball is moving toward them) and movement (how the ball sinks, rises, or curves inward or outward). Ron had, himself, devised a third factor.

Nearly every pitching coach will teach a pitcher to stand and pitch from the exact same spot on the mound. Consistency leads to accuracy, after all. But Ron mused, *What if I throw pitches from all different locations on the mound, effectively adding another complication for batters to have to contend with?*

Ron changed his game. It was speed, movement, and his location as a pitcher that now mattered most. With fluidity, athleticism, and innovation, he kept one foot at all times on the twenty-four-inch "rubber" on the mound but moved with each pitch, throwing heat from all angles. Ron became unhittable.

And coaches and scouts began to notice.

As he approached his eighteenth birthday, he received a surprise call. It was a once-in-a-lifetime offer for someone with his passion: a contract with the Cleveland Indians' triple A baseball team. Seventeen years old, and Ron had an offer. It was a dream. His dream. He excitedly called his father, who would need to sign the contract for his then minor son.

"No," his father said. "Baseball is a game. You're going to get a real job. You need, in fact, to join me in our family business. And that is exactly what you will do."

And that is exactly what Ron did.

He worked in his family's women's clothing business for years. When it failed under the competitive weight of newer, larger, more efficient manufacturers, he tried to find other innovative ways to design and sell sweaters and dresses. But the passion was never really there.

As Ron and I looked at each other, in the middle of the hubbub of my aunt's dining room, me leaning toward him in his wheelchair and him looking at me with his piercing blue eyes, Ron set his hand on mine.

"I have regretted that day for my entire life," he said. "I'm ninety-four, and I have thought about that contract every single day since." In that moment, it felt as if the party, the house, the festivities had all dissolved. It was just Ron and me.

He leaned toward me and said, "Do what you love to do. Promise me, Scott—do what you love to do."

. . .

What do *you* love to do?

What inhabits your daydreams' sunlit moments, the seconds before your head leaves the morning pillow? What do you really desire before you have time to be cognizant of whether it's practical? It's a simple question with a too-often daunting answer.

Let me clarify: What would you love to do if money were absolutely no object and your work were valued by how it betters the lives of other people? Does that change your answer?

Now, an uncomfortable question: How would you feel if I told you that the work you are doing right now is the work that you have to do for the rest of your life? Would you be relieved, thrilled, terrified?

Back in the 1990s, I had a colleague who worked at the top of our field in high-level fundraising. He worked with donors and philanthropists at the highest levels of impact and sophistication. He had a master's degree, he was charismatic, and he was rapidly climbing the rungs of our professional ladder. The work was high stress, high profile, and well compensated. And then one day, I heard that he'd quit to be a kindergarten teacher.

Truthfully, I was taken aback, focusing totally on all that he'd just "given up."

Just a couple of years later, he was by far the most sought-after teacher in a highly prestigious school system. The kids absolutely loved him, and so did the parents and teachers.

The Courage to Dream Big

Dare to dream, then decide to do. —ANNETTE WHITE

Work is the crucible in which our best selves meet an imperfect world.

Despite the realities of budgets, schedules, and bosses, work should be where we bring our full beings—our hands, our minds, our ideas, our energy. Work should be a tool for creation, for innovation. A place that challenges us to think on our feet, to grapple with goals previously unimaginable, to collaborate with people we may or may not like, and to be inventive in ways our personal lives don't demand.

Today—yes, *today*—you can, through force of will, concept, or personality, bring an idea into fruition in this world. Work is the vehicle. (For some of you, "work" is being a full-time parent, a volunteer, a retiree who craves to make an impact. Please know that this chapter is absolutely meant for you, too!)

And yet, so many are drifting. Floating along in their comfort zones.

Most of us will spend at least ninety thousand hours working over the course of our careers (and even more if we work past the age of sixty-five), and statistics show that many of us are either massively stressed at work or completely checked out. Nearly 60 percent of employees in a 2021 Gallup poll felt intense work-related stress on a daily basis, and a 2013 study indicated that less than one-third of American workers felt engaged at their jobs.

Even more worrisome, nearly 20 percent were "actively disengaged."

Sleepwalking through life. Picking up the paycheck every two weeks and biding time. Viewing work through the outdated prism of "have to" or "this is what I know." Or being buffeted by the winds of inner fears: "What will people think of me if I quit?" "I can't do that—it isn't prestigious enough," or "What if I fail and suffer from a lifetime of regret?"

In 2005, the late author David Foster Wallace delivered a commencement address—commonly referred to as his "This Is Water" speech—to Kenyon College's newly minted graduates. He told the following story:

> There are these two young fish swimming along and they happen to meet an older fish swimming the other way, who nods at them and says "Morning, boys. How's the water?" And the two young fish swim on for a bit, and then eventually one of them looks over at the other and goes "What the hell is water?"

For many, our work is like water: we've been working for so long we've forgotten exactly why we are in it at all. Now is your opportunity to remember exactly what you love to do. And take the scary steps to do it.

To be sure, there are hundreds of books that have been written about motivation, career coaching, business models, and new modes of post-pandemic hybrid work life; this chapter does not aim to summarize or challenge them. What this chapter does, rather, is ask you to take a hard, scary, complex look at what you do, why you are doing it, and what it would look like if your work matched the passionate adventure of a life you want to lead.

I know that for many, economic needs are real and that you need your current work to survive. This is not about quitting your job, resigning, walking away, or selling your company. Unless you want to, of course. And for many, parenting is your beyond-full-time work. This chapter is about courageously thinking, asking, and acting in a way that will enlighten you as to who you are, what you're great at, and what is most meaningful to you.

Yes, it will all take courage. And let's dream big.

Insight Exercise: Getting Back to the Work We Love

Here are some questions designed to get your juices flowing! Grab a journal and spend some time reflecting on your work (or family/volunteer) life right now:

1. *Do you currently possess the mindset of playing it safe or the mindset of taking risks?*
2. *If you dislike what you do on a daily basis, what is stopping you from changing it?*
3. *What price are you willing to pay for financial success? Would you be willing to do something you hate for a big paycheck?*
4. *What were you taught when you were young about the responsibilities of work? Do any of those beliefs still inform your mindset today?*

Swan Takes the Big Leap

Career decisions are always hard. Even more so when they make you question your entire identity and self-worth.

I had what most would consider a successful career in the corporate world. Having led digital marketing globally for companies like Nike, Revlon, and Estée Lauder, and with institutions like Bain, Harvard, and Columbia under my belt, I was proud of my accomplishments. I felt seen, validated, and respected.

That seed was planted from a young age. My parents didn't have the privilege of attending high school and worked multiple jobs, so academics was imperative in our Asian tiger-parent household. An A-minus was an Asian F, and Harvard was the only option. An immigrant kid to the US, I rocked the standard-issue bowl haircut and big purple glasses and talked incessantly about space exploration. Needless to say, I didn't have a lot of friends, so I leaned even further into achievement. It became a goal inseparable from my identity—my safety blanket. That continued well into the corporate world, as I built a textbook resume. I secretly felt pride when people asked about my job or alma mater, and I was rewarded with due respect. It served me well, getting me progressively better roles and bigger stages worldwide. I thought I'd played it all right.

A few years ago, I landed everyone's dream job with one of the best brands in the world, a household name in every single country. I was running the largest team I'd ever helmed. I got thousands of congratulatory messages. It was perfect—the ultimate reward for a career's worth of hard work. I should have been elated. This should have fed my inner achievement monster beyond my wildest dreams. Yet nothing fit. The culture, people, function, location—this was meant to be my forever job, and I was miserable every day. It was hard to get up for work in the mornings. Hard to walk into meetings and not feel like an outsider or imposter. I wasn't performing to half of my potential. But overachievers don't quit!

The irony is this isn't a story about leaving. That was inevitable. But it was the aftermath of the decision that was even harder. It was the first time I'd finished a role without another lined up, and the ambiguity was debilitating. Was I really any good at this? What happens without a steady paycheck, especially as I've sent money home to my family every month since college? Floating, searching, and without a title to introduce myself with, who was I, and what was my contribution to society?

I was lost, and it was the best thing that could have happened to me. To be asked, "What do you do?" and to answer, "I don't know," feels naked and vulnerable. But I sat with it. I stared it in the face and asked the tough questions with no one else around (one thing they don't tell you when you leave the corporate world—when you don't have brand budgets or access to parties anymore—you learn who your real friends are). I could no longer draw my self-worth from my titles and accomplishments. I was forced to figure out who I really was and my purpose in this world.

Origin stories. That fragile inner child is who we protect, even as we grow into successful, confident adults. I would probably have learned to code or gone to space if I'd thought it was possible, but I had no reference. My purpose crystalized so clearly: to democratize information and access in ways I'd never had.

Four months later, I got on my first public company board, being decades younger than my peers, and then another. I advise a VC and a SPAC. I own an energy drink with teenage TikTok influencers. And the craziest shift: I went from corporate to creator, with millions of followers. I create content on anything I desire, unfiltered and honest. I've had the honor of interviewing people from Paris Hilton and Floyd Mayweather to the founders of Netflix, Android, and Twitch. On my live shows, I've given away internships, startup funding, and recording contracts. For this, *Forbes* dubbed me the "Queen of

Clubhouse." I get to help shape the future of web3 and how we live and play. I now fully pursue curiosity without regard to achievement, but the latter has followed in spades. And every day, I tell the world I still have no idea what I want to be when I grow up.

Twenty Years of Yesterdays

If you have knowledge, let others light their candles in it.

—MARGARET FULLER

Consider these two scenarios:

The alarm on Steve's phone chimes loudly. Steve moans and rolls over, frowning as he looks at the time: 7:00 a.m. "Just ten more minutes," he effortlessly persuades himself, and he taps the snooze button, pulling the covers back over his head.

After two more snooze sessions, Steve finally, begrudgingly, pulls himself out of bed and toward the shower. On the way, he picks up his phone and begins reading his emails. His blood pressure increases as he sees an email from a new colleague who is hoping to get some time on his calendar. "Can't he figure this crap out on his own? I have enough damn stuff to do myself."

His scrolling stops at a calendar invite for today's presentation about a new company initiative. He's already dreading it. He knows everyone will have an opinion, and frankly, he doesn't care whether it happens anyway. *Just another dog-and-pony show*, he thinks.

On his way to the train station, he takes time to stop off at a donut shop for his usual: a glazed cruller and extra-large coffee. Pulling his car into the station lot, he hustles to make the train. Twenty minutes later, he and dozens of others, heads down, peering at their phones as they walk, disembark and trudge toward another day.

Just like yesterday. And twenty years of yesterdays.

Same morning…same company…and Sue's old-school alarm clock chimes loudly.

Sue looks at the time and feels a swell of pride. It's 5:45 a.m. She's not a morning person by any means but has grown to love waking early and starting her day. She places her feet firmly on the floor, steadying herself. When she rises, she takes the opportunity to breathe deeply as she makes her bed.

She sits for several minutes by her bedroom window, darkness still outlining the trees. She closes her eyes, getting centered and focused for the day. After ten minutes, she reaches for her journal, which is sitting on the windowsill as always. She jots down a few thoughts and then reviews her to-do list for the day. She has a meeting with a new hire. This makes her smile; she loves seeing the understanding that blooms when someone starts to "get it," and she revels in her role of being a mentor at work. She's also making a presentation about a new company initiative and is excited to share her ideas and get feedback; she's passionate about the potential, and today is the day to make it happen.

After a quick shower, she dresses, drinks a smoothie, throws her laptop into her backpack, and heads out. Last year, she started biking to work. Some of her most innovative ideas have come from this moving communion of exercise and contemplation.

An hour later, she strides through the front doors. She's energized and prepared. After twenty years, Sue still loves what she does. More than ever, actually.

Same morning…two different people…and two different perspectives on the role of work in their lives.

Here's a question: *In which one do you see more of yourself?*

Insight Exercise: Assessing Your Current Work Life

Think back for a minute. Why are you doing the work you are doing now?

- Did you choose it out of a passion that still exists today?
- Did you take a job because someone expected you to?
- Do you need to do this job (or multiple jobs) because you need to provide for yourself or your family?
- Did you take the job for the money and now maybe feel stuck or trapped?
- Did you get comfortable, and are you afraid to tempt failure by trying something else?
- Do you, in some way, feel flawed and not deserving of different, better work?
- Do you feel, in some way, that changing jobs would reflect badly on others who wish to stay?

Take some time to react to this: Would you choose it if you had to do it all over again?

_____

_____

_____

Now, reflect on and respond to these seven statements, circling the corresponding number, with 1 being the lowest score and 10 the highest:

1. I feel really clear about my responsibilities in my job.

    1—2—3—4—5—6—7—8—9—10

2. I am really making an impact on others (or the business) in a way that is meaningful to me.

    1—2—3—4—5—6—7—8—9—10

3. I freely share my opinions and ideas on the job.

   1—2—3—4—5—6—7—8—9—10

4. I generally feel engaged in and excited by my work.

   1—2—3—4—5—6—7—8—9—10

5. At work, I am viewed as an expert in at least one aspect of what I do.

   1—2—3—4—5—6—7—8—9—10

6. I generally enjoy relationships with my fellow co-workers.

   1—2—3—4—5—6—7—8—9—10

7. I am currently in my dream job.

   1—2—3—4—5—6—7—8—9—10

OK, add up your scores: _____ Now, divide by seven: _____

- If your average is 8.5 to 10, you are living your personal legend. Your career is exciting, impactful, fulfilling.
- If your average is 7 to 8.4, you are in a good zone, but there is work to do in either finding more meaning or impact in your work, or adding new avenues for that in your life.
- If your average is 6 to 6.9, your work is not as fulfilling as it could be. It's time to think about how to create some real change.
- If your average is 5.9 or below, it's time to reflect on what about your job can be changed, what you can do to change your own mindset, or whether it's time to take a big leap to something else.

_____

_____

_____

Let's think about what you've discovered. Are you surprised at how you spend your time and how you rank your job satisfaction? What did you learn that you didn't know before this exercise?

Very importantly, let's see how your values align with your work. Take a look back to your Audacious Courage Manifesto and write down your five most important values:

1. _____

2. _____

3. _____

4. _____

5. _____

Now think: Do these values sync with what you actually do in your work, and what is one shift that you can make right now that will help your work align more with your values?

_____

_____

_____

The Greatest (and Dirtiest) Job I Ever Had

The world is full of magic things, patiently waiting for our senses to grow sharper. —W. B. YEATS

I've had all kinds of jobs in my life: real estate developer, divorce coach, strategic planner, pharmacy stock boy, hotel bellboy, concert ticket runner, alternative music expert at an old-school record store. But there's one job that gave me the most visceral sense of what I need to accomplish in this world:

It was being an egg farmer.

On Kibbutz Tzuba, on the outskirts of Jerusalem, my job, along with my work partner Igor, was to don a dusty blue work outfit and enter one of five large chicken houses. Each chaotic, noisy coop was full of twenty thousand chickens in various stages of squawking, strutting, fighting, and, on occasion, laying eggs.

The work was dirty and tiring.

The smell was…well, you can guess.

Starting before sunrise, Igor and I would open large wooden bins filled with sawdust and reach under the unhappy fowl to collect their eggs, constantly catching sawdust in our eyes and enduring beak and talon scrapes across our arms. The work was hard, but I was actually really good at it; in fact, I became a bit of an expert.

I started to take pride in how efficiently I could work; I created games and challenges for myself to see how fast I could collect the bounty with breaking the fewest possible eggs.

I grew close to Igor. We connected and formed our own unbeatable egg-collecting team.

And one calm morning at sunrise, it hit me.

I had already been on the job for hours, and I was walking with two huge buckets full of freshly laid eggs to the kibbutz's dining hall in preparation for the daily communal breakfast. As I handed the eggs to the cook standing by his grill, I realized that my work that morning would help to feed the community. That sustenance would then fuel them in their collective work. It was a cycle, one in which I played a small, yet essential part.

As crazy as it may sound, I felt in service to that community. I felt connected. A wave of joy washed over me. And even crazier yet, as I stood there in my dirty blue uniform, my boots muddy, feathers coming out of my pockets, I knew that the job had taught me something powerful:

To be happy and fulfilled, I needed to live a life dedicated to service—one in which I strive to make people's lives better.

Ever since then, through every career I have had, that commitment—born in the chicken coop—has been my North Star.

Scare Your Soul Challenge: Take One "Scary" Action Toward More Meaningful Work

Think of what you have accomplished in this chapter! First, you reflected deeply and courageously on the nature of your work, what you love about it, and the mindset you bring. You were open and honest with yourself about what's working…and what isn't.

You went back to why you started your current role in the first place. Maybe that wasn't so comfortable to confront. Restate that rationale here:

_____

_____

You took time to rate your current work life based on clarity, meaning, ability to share your ideas, and more. Write your score again here: _____

You returned to your values and reflected on whether they align with your current work. What was one values-based shift you chose to make?

_____

_____

Now that you have done all the heavy lifting, you're ready to make some scary shifts. And only you know what leap you need to take. Do you need to leave the corporate world to pursue your art? Do you need to start that side hustle you are passionate about? Do you need to quit your job and start your own company? Do you need to step up and demand more responsibility, pay, autonomy? Do you love what you do and want to start mentoring or guiding others? Or maybe your shift is small but still pushes you. Only you know. Only you can commit to it. So...

What is one "scary" step you will commit to taking that will make your work life zing with greater passion? The kind of passion that you KNOW you can have and deserve.

So, what's it going to be?

_____

_____

_____

Key Insights

1. Work is the crucible in which our best efforts meet an imperfect world. Whether we are lawyers, teachers, farmers, actuaries, painters, politicians, hedge fund managers, sheet metal workers...our work is where we use our innate gifts to alter the world around us.

2. Despite the importance of work—and the vast amount of our lives we dedicate to it—so many are not engaged, feel stressed, and otherwise are not living a fulfilling work life.

3. Diving deep into our work with clear, open eyes allows us to see what we typically don't: how we really feel about our work, what gives us enthusiasm and love, what aligns with our values, and what we would really want to do if money was no object. This is the foundation from which we can take bold action moving forward.

Moving Forward

The Journey Ahead

CHAPTER 15

Those Who Go the Hard Way with Us

> An honorable human relationship—that is, one in which two people have the right to use the word "love"—is a process, delicate, violent, often terrifying to both persons involved, a process of refining the truths they can tell each other. It is important to do this because it breaks down human self-delusion and isolation. It is important to do this because in doing so we do justice to our own complexity. It is important to do this because we can count on so few people to go that hard way with us. —ADRIENNE RICH

The day Laura and I finalized our divorce was sunny and cold.

After five years of marriage and two kids, we knew it was time. We waited—just the two of us—on a bench in a sterile hallway deep within Cuyahoga County's courthouse. Finally, the magistrate called us into a small office. Two documents and pens lay on either side of a conference table. Laura and I took our seats.

Together, we read over each page of the legal directive, my mind drifting back to happier times: our wedding day's fanfare, the jubilant guests, the dancing, the klezmer band, my friends extolling the virtues of the icy cold shots that exited an ice sculpture they called the "vodka luge."

Not long after we married, Laura and I welcomed one child and then another into our family. At the courthouse that day, I remembered the wobbly and impossibly exciting first steps; the love and second-guessing and companionship of parenting alongside Laura; our son Noah's first-birthday balloons we watched float in a tangle into the autumn sky.

And then, with no more fanfare than two quick signatures, it was done. On the way out, we shared a sad hug and then ventured out separately into the cold sunshine.

By the time I got back to my car, I had an overwhelming need for those who knew me best. I put my car into gear, and almost on autopilot, I drove to my people. Straight home.

My parents, once young coeds, were now in their sixties. I was thirty-six years old, no longer a child. And yet, there they were, waiting for me at their door, *still* my parents.

We sat in their small den with the soft gray felt wallpaper. It was the same room where, as a child with mononucleosis, I sipped ginger ale for days. Where we would laugh at my French bulldog, Morty, as he stood guard on the edge of the couch, enraptured by squirrels outside the window. Where we toasted my return home from far-off adventures. Where we cried together. Now we talked about life, about love. About starting new chapters. And with family support, I was wonderfully ready for the life in front of me.

• • •

So, who are *your* people?

If the social order of your life were mapped on the trunk of a newly felled tree, who would be in your innermost ring? What do they do for you in times of need? How do they support you? And how can you engage them even more?

This chapter focuses on finding and engaging the people and community who will support us in our Scare Your Soul work. They'll understand our need to take risks while building exceptional lives.

They'll support decisions that engender both change and uncertainty. They'll be copilots as we embark on scary but meaningful work.

They'll be our ride-or-dies, no matter what.

Of Choirs and Catalysts

Set your life on fire. Seek those who fan your flames. —RUMI

I have had the honor to work with and learn from many wise and generous teachers. Some have transcended that role and become mentors. One of the wisest is Maria Sirois.

To be in Maria's presence is to be gifted with a sense of timelessness. Maria has worked for decades with families raising children with terminal illness. She's a uniquely present listener. Her TEDx Talk entitled "Living an Authentic Life" is brilliant and powerful.

The first time I ever saw Maria, I sat rapt in a large audience of positive psychology students. Her long silver hair glowed in the spotlight. Maria spoke deliberately, savoring each and every syllable of a Rumi poem's delicious ending, "come, even if you have broken your vow a hundred times. Come again, come."

Over the years, Maria has taken a special seat in my life. She has voiced—through her own good intuition and judgment—how I am strong enough to venture on when I'm afraid. Maria has been a catalyst for me, a person who inspires me to serve others as she serves, to teach people how to better connect and listen.

Maria Sirois beautifully designates the group of people who offer this type of unconditional love our "choir."

The Conversation in Dharamsala

My humanity is bound up in yours, for we can only be human together. —DESMOND TUTU

A moment of the power of connection that I return to often is a delicious peek offered into the friendship between two of the world's greatest teachers.

The Dalai Lama and Archbishop Desmond Tutu visited the Tibetan Children's Village in the spring of 2015, in Dharamsala, India.

A group of Tibetan leaders founded the Upper Tibetan Children's Village in 1960 for the purpose of providing refuge to fifty-one Tibetan orphans. Those orphans had been doubly displaced: they'd lost their home country and their families. In the aftermath of those twin tragedies, the school's founding leaders knew that the children needed not only an education, but love and friendship.

By the time of the Dalai Lama and Tutu's visit, over one thousand children called the school their home. Despite their differences, and over the span of fifty-five years, the Village School's students present and past had binding similarities: They'd had to leave their homes in Tibet forever. And most likely, they would not see their families again.

Both of their guests that day had famously faced hardship. Both had experienced decades of oppression, personally and on behalf of their people. Both had distinguished themselves as moral icons by what they learned from their struggles. And maybe it was due to their sense of shared struggle—on behalf of their beloved Tibetan and South African people—that the two had become dear friends. As captured by directors Peggy Callahan and Louie Psihoyos in their brilliant documentary *MISSION: JOY—Finding Happiness in Troubled Times*, the Dalai Lama and Tutu's trip to the school would provide a unique and unanticipated glimpse into their psyches.

Upon their arrival, the pair were first escorted into the school's small library. Smiling, they took their seats in armchairs amidst the well-organized bookshelves and library walls festooned with brightly colored school projects. The Dalai Lama sat in his maroon robes with a deep-gold stripe, Tutu in a slightly rumpled gray suit, bright-purple shirt, a white linen scarf around his shoulders, and a large gold cross that dangled down across his belly. One by one, several girls and boys shared details of the heartbreaking loss encountered in their journeys from Tibet.

Finally, a young girl in a grass-colored dress stepped forward. After greeting the two guests, she said simply, "I was only five when I had to leave my family behind." She continued, "The pain I felt leaving my family…" But her voice trailed off as she, overcome by emotion, dissolved into tears. The room went silent. Archbishop Tutu's daughter, Mpho, who was standing nearby, went to the girl's side and hugged her as she wept.

After a pause, these two men—two of the most influential moral leaders in modern world history—spoke.

Tutu offered a simple, loving affirmation. "Sorry," he said, almost in a whisper.

The Dalai Lama held his palms together and raised them to his face for a moment, seemingly deep in reflection.

"Now you should think at present you've got complete freedom," he finally said, firmly. "And have the opportunity to study not only modern education, but to study, learning our ancient thousand-year-old rich culture."

On that day in April, Tutu and the Dalai Lama articulated the very ingredients that I believe support us as we continue the effort of pushing comfort zones and tackling fears.

1. Tutu embodied a message of sincere, uncompromising love—the kind of love that has no barriers, no criteria. The people who provide that kind of grounding, unconditional love are our "choirs."

2. The Dalai Lama embodied a message of courage. He firmly articulated what we can be, and what we must do. The people who provide that insight to you and me are our "catalysts."

Hearing Our Choirs Sing

*I would rather walk with a friend in the dark, than alone in
the light.* —HELEN KELLER

We often tell ourselves that, in moments of challenge, we have to
go it alone. For some, asking for support from others demonstrates
weakness. We may think the following:

- *I don't want to burden others with my problems.*
- *People have enough going on in their own lives.*
- *My fears are mine; I should keep them that way.*
- *People will never understand what I'm going through anyway.*
- *I am going to embarrass myself.*
- *If I share my struggle, it will be obvious that I have no idea what
  I'm doing.*
- *I don't want to give negative feelings airtime.*
- *I don't deserve love and support.*
- *I don't know who loves me.*

But choirs are there for us no matter what. They see our flaws,
quirks, and imperfections as part of our unique mosaic.

Choirs are composed of those people you call at 2:00 a.m. when
you desperately need a ride from the airport. They are also whom
you call at 2:00 p.m. to celebrate the big win you just had at work.

And the size and composition of our choirs change over time. Life
transitions, in particular—moving to new cities, starting new jobs,
getting married, having children, pursuing new hobbies, having major
adventures, getting divorced, empty nesting, retiring—often add to or
subtract from our choirs.

Over time, I've learned that we don't need a big choir. (We actually only really need one good friend in life.) What matters is our

commitment to identifying them, showing them appreciation, and calling on them when fear strikes our hearts and stops us from doing the things we truly need to do.

Scare Your Soul Challenge: Rediscovering Your Choir

Take some time and think about who loves you unconditionally. Who's in your corner no matter what? Now, list them on a sheet of paper. (If you don't have anyone in your choir, add one very important person to the list: *you*.)

Now, I invite you to courageously show your choir your appreciation. Even doing this can sometimes be scary. We don't typically pick up the phone and call someone for the express purpose of telling them that we love them and appreciate them. Sometimes, we let it remain unsaid. Not today.

Take some time to reach out to every member of your choir and express your gratitude and appreciation to them. Here are some suggestions of what you might say:

- *Thank you for everything you've done for me. I am the person I am today in part because of you.*
- *Thank you for always being loyal and always having my back. Please know that I will always have yours.*
- *I have some wonderful friends in my life, but you are a "forever friend."*
- *Thank you for seeing me—with all of my flaws and quirks—and still loving me. Your love gives me strength to venture courageously into the world.*
- *Thank you for enhancing my creativity, my drive, my passion, which allows me to be my best.*

Finally, take a moment to reflect. How did you feel when you listed your choir? Powerful, emboldened, comforted, sad? Describe it here:

_____

_____

_____

And what happened when you showed appreciation to your choir? How did they react? What did they say? How did it feel for you in the moment?

Danielle Makes a Decision

Had I been looking in a genetic mirror the entire time I cared for my mom? That was the question running through my head as I watched my beautiful fifty-five-year-old mom starve herself to death as she took control of her destiny with Huntington's disease.

HD is known as a "family disease" because every child of a parent with HD has a fifty-fifty chance of inheriting the fatal gene for this progressive brain disorder that causes uncontrolled movements, emotional problems, and loss of thinking ability (cognition). If the gene is passed down, the children will 100 percent get the disease at some point in their lifetime. Back in the day, they called it the "devil's disease." Today, there are approximately forty-one thousand symptomatic Americans and more than two hundred thousand at risk of inheriting. Most people choose not to get tested, because there isn't a cure yet.

For me, knowledge is power. I knew I couldn't fully mourn my mom's death or move on with my life until I knew my own genetic status. So, three months after my mom died, I started the process of genetic counseling and testing. The test itself was simple—a quick blood draw. Waiting for the results was agonizing.

Am I strong enough to handle this type of information? Will anyone want to marry me? Will I ever have kids? Will I ever get to experience everything that I want to if my time on this earth is limited? How much information is too much information and what information is correct? Should I end my own life before things get too bad? These were the questions that consumed me.

Three weeks after the blood draw, I walked into my neurologist's office to get my results. As soon as I saw the look on my doctor's face, I knew that I was the next generation of HD in my family. I didn't cry right away. I was numb for months and certainly tried to run away from my problems for a few years. I drank, I cried, I became depressed, and I kept myself so busy that I couldn't even think straight.

Two years later, I had to make a similar decision, but this one wasn't just for me—it was for my baby and her future. I had always thought that I would be the last generation of HD in my family, so after an unplanned pregnancy, my only option was to go through chorionic villus sampling to learn if my baby had HD. With the same doctors by my side, I went through the process again. This time, the excitement on my doctor's face told me that my daughter would never have to worry about Huntington's disease.

Now, seven years later, I'm still confident in my decision to get tested. I still believe in the power of knowledge and work hard every day to be the strong person that my daughter would be proud of. I managed to redirect my anger and depression and put it toward something positive. Therapy, travel, and advocacy have become an important part of my life. I'm married, we have an HD-negative baby, and I have an amazing support system of doctors, friends, and family. Sure, I still have days where I'm paralyzed by what my future might look like, but I can finally look back and say that I made it through the storm. It reminds me of a favorite quote from Haruki Murakami: "Once the storm is over, you won't remember how

> you made it through, how you managed to survive. You won't even be sure whether the storm is over. But one thing is for certain, when you come out of the storm, you won't be the same person who walked in. That's what the storm is all about."

Calling All Catalysts

If you want to go quickly, go alone. If you want to go far, go together. —AFRICAN PROVERB

It was between my pasta dinner and the tiramisu dessert that Susan shot me a look. I knew what she wanted.

We were out for dinner with my dear friends Jen and Dan. I'd told Susan about an idea I'd been toying with for weeks and couldn't stop thinking about. Now, as she looked keenly at me, I could tell that she wanted me to share it. So, as dessert arrived, I told Jen and Dan about my idea for creating a "happiness incubator."

From my own childhood—when I'd found it difficult to connect with people outside of my family—I knew how loneliness felt. I'd tirelessly researched the data—from Robert Waldinger's Harvard longitudinal study and others—that confirmed that connecting people helps combat isolation and its resulting diseases, depression and anxiety. I believed that there had to be a way to bring both pleasure and meaning into people's lives and to do so in courageous, boundary-pushing ways. I felt that we could create surprising and connecting experiences.

I still had a lot of open questions, but I'd already devised a name—Thrive.

By the time we paid our bill and walked out into the night air, Jen—a brilliant strategist with extensive experience with positive organizational development and international social work—was on board to be my fifty-fifty partner.

Jen's and my know-how got Thrive going. But the catalysts for its success—the secret sauce—were the intrepid, creative, and gutsy volunteers that Jen and I recruited into our joy circus. Their professions were as varied as their personalities: the team boasted an architect, a nurse, an environmental activist, a photographer, a social media manager, a furniture maker, a chef, a greeting card company executive, a trucking company dispatcher, and many more.

Thrive's mission was direct: harness the creativity and passion of our collective to create surprising, boundary-pushing, sometimes-wacky experiences to delight and inspire. And delight and inspire we did. Our planning primarily took place during engaging potluck dinners at my house. We began with simple ideas, teasing them out until they became fully formed communal experiences. Over the next several years, our volunteer team planned and led events that made a big splash:

- Noontime, intergenerational dance parties with a well-known DJ
- A "flash parade," which ran through a busy office building and a college campus
- A surprise multi-instrument drum circle and a wild "silent disco" rave in a contemporary art museum
- An event featuring cocktails and spandex-clad ninjas (why not?) focused on authentic communication
- Gratitude murals as a canvas for public expressions of thankfulness
- A surprise wedding for two high school sweethearts

Our work with Thrive caught the attention of the local leaders of TEDx—Eric and Hallie Kogelschatz. They wanted to know if we would consider giving a TEDx Talk. In fact, they wondered whether we'd give the final talk of a conference, culminating a day full of dynamic and influential speakers.

We accepted immediately.

Those Who Lift Us Higher

> I've learned that people will forget what you said, people
> will forget what you did, but people will never forget how
> you made them feel. —MAYA ANGELOU

Soon after, I received a call from Maria Sirois, my old friend, mentor, and catalyst. Upon hearing about the opportunity TEDx had given Thrive, she congratulated me and then insisted that she fly in from Boston the week before to coach Jen and me. She wouldn't be able to stay for the talk but wanted to help us make this opportunity everything it could be, courtesy of "Boot Camp Maria."

We sat for hours in Jen's living room while Maria coached us. Although we were already on version ten of our script, she unabashedly challenged our thinking. She asked tough questions. She made us think deeper. Our script improved.

Maria then helped us navigate the talk's complex structure: two of us would be speaking and we would need to coordinate our timing; we would be holding a surprise DJ-led rave in the middle of the talk (we would be hiding hundreds of glow sticks beneath the chairs in the audience for the moment); and importantly, our talk hinged on thirty-seven images that would flash on an enormous screen behind us. Getting used to the handheld clicker to trigger those images would be critical.

With the script down and the order of the talk set, Maria counseled that the key to our success would be constant repetition. We would need to know the talk backward and forward. And that is just what we did, repeating the fifteen-minute talk again and again. We smoothed out every syllabic "um" and "so" like a hot iron on a damp shirt.

When we finally had it memorized, we began again, but this time scrolling (via the handheld clicker) through the thirty-seven images that would make our talk. The images included exuberant photos from our events, compelling research data, and other shots that would really bring our talk to life. But each time I tried, I screwed up. I'd forget to click the slide or messed up the timing. I was frustrated and embarrassed. But Maria urged me on. We repeated and repeated until, yes, finally, I got the clicker and the timing down.

On Maria's departure day, we hugged and said goodbye. As we did, Jen and I knew it: we were ready.

On the day of the talk, I dressed in the outfit I'd chosen so carefully: dark jeans (I figured one had to appear effortlessly casual in TED Talks), a gray shirt and pocket square, a cool blue blazer, and tan shoes buffed to a fine shine. As we sat in the greenroom with the other speakers, we noticed a large carefully wrapped item (a casket?) being rolled in on a dolly by two beefy security guards.

Yoko Ono, it would turn out, had personally approved the appearance of a special item that would be used in the TEDx Talk before ours. My mind raced back to my early days in Joan Silberbach's art class when I heard what it was: John Lennon's most famous guitar.

The guards held all of us speakers at bay, not allowing us to even get close.

As the speaker before us—the CEO of the Rock and Roll Hall of Fame and Museum—began his talk, Jen and I parted; she headed to stage right and I headed toward a small dark hallway on stage left. Alone in the dim light, I waited. Then I noticed it. Four feet away from me sat John Lennon's guitar, solitary on a guitar stand.

Visions of the scene in which Christopher Guest admonishes Rob Reiner for touching his guitar in the 1984 movie *This Is Spinal Tap* ("No, don't touch it…don't point…don't even look at it") crept into my head. But there it was. I looked around. I inched closer, heart beating fast, standing just near enough that I could almost feel my idol's presence.

It was in that haze of musical reminiscence that I made my rookie mistake. When it was my time, I walked out onto the stage having forgotten to take the clicker from the stage manager.

It was one minute and fifty-two seconds into the talk when I felt the odd emptiness in my left hand. My mind raced. *Where could the clicker be? What am I going to do?* I wanted to run or to somehow travel back in time and remember to take the clicker. Seven hundred faces looked up at me, my mind tipping toward oblivion.

Then I thought of Maria. And instinct kicked in.

All of Maria's training, the countless times she held us accountable to repeat that script—I remembered I knew the talk so well. I allowed my brain to slow down, process the task in front of me, and devise a plan. I figured the clicker would most probably be backstage, and, if well-timed, I could slink backward into the shadows, grab it, and be back onstage by the time Jen finished the first segment of her remarks.

In what may be one of the greatest moments of relief in my life, as I slipped backstage, the stage manager barreled down the dim hallway toward me, clicker in hand.

The rest of the talk was pure pleasure.

I felt comfortable, even joyous. Jen was spectacular. Halfway through, we surprised the attendees with the appearance of our DJ—Steph Floss—who kicked into Montell Jordan's "This Is How We Do It." The entire audience rose to their feet in our impromptu TEDx dance party.

I leapt off the stage and into the first row and began dancing among them. And I thought of Maria, my catalyst, who helped raise me higher. With glow sticks waving throughout the huge hall, we did the only thing that felt right and true in that moment.

We all just danced.

Scare Your Soul Challenge: The Catalyst Praise Shower

Bring to mind one person who raises you up.

What is your history together? Why do you love them so much? Are you sure that they know how you feel about them? Is there something that you can do right now that would help them in some way?

Take one small action—it could be bravely reading a list of their attributes or mailing them a letter showcasing the list. The key:

shower them with authentic praise. Let them know that you are a proud member of their choir and always will be.

Now, let's get even scarier and bolder...and flip the script.

Think of one person in your life—and you don't have to know them well—whom you could raise up.

Is there someone you could mentor or provide with expertise? Don't wait for them to call you; proactively reach out to them and let them know that they indeed have tremendous promise. You see it! And you want to help.

Offer up yourself fully, with no expectation of reward other than serving as a catalyst for someone else. Take the initiative.

Key Insights

1. We can always fly solo through life, but as social animals, we all crave connection, support, and belonging. In the process of leading a courageous life, we benefit by having support systems around us. Often, we don't think about these individuals until a crisis hits; or we don't take the time to thank and appreciate them. But they are near to our hearts, and identifying, thanking, and involving them makes the journey better.

2. Our choir is composed of the ride-or-dies in our lives who will love us no matter what. Oftentimes, our choirs can feel smaller than we would like; but in this case, it's quality over quantity. Science says we only really need one good friend to be markedly happier.

3. Our catalysts are those who raise us up, challenge us, make us better. They may reside in our choirs, but their role is to be additive to what we do and who we are becoming. Just as critical is our role as a catalyst for others as a mentor or guide. It can be just as meaningful as any relationship we will have, and often, it begins with something as simple as a phone call.

CHAPTER 16

The Journey Ahead

There is a candle in your heart, ready to be kindled. There is
a void in your soul, ready to be filled. You feel it, don't you?

—RUMI

There is a long tradition of loved ones writing letters and slipping them
into travelers' rucksacks or steamer trunks. Equally vital were the letters that the journeyer would leave behind as the front door closed quietly behind them.

Letters are time machines.

They mark a moment. The words—indelible in handwriting—
trace a map of thoughts and intentions from the heart and head
onto the page.

One afternoon, in a quiet home in Arnold, Missouri, Donna
Gregory found such a letter.

In this small town of twenty thousand on the far northern lip
of the Mark Twain National Forest, she and her then husband were
busy packing up his deceased grandparents' home. In the darkened
back corner of a bedroom closet, she saw a box.

It contained, among other things, a high school diploma, news clip-
pings, dog tags, and medals belonging to someone neither Donna nor
her husband had ever heard of: one army private first class John Farrell
Eddington. Among the cache—which also included a Purple Heart—
was written notification from the War Department that Eddington
had been killed in action more than five decades earlier, in June 1944.

And then there was the letter.

Private Eddington had penned the missive to his then three-week-old daughter, Peggy. The letter had a Texas postmark, where Private Eddington had been deep in basic training. He would never actually meet his daughter, as he would die in Italy just four months after the letter was mailed.

Donna Gregory read it over and over as she and her husband drove the eighteen miles back to their home in St. Louis. It was there that she began researching. She wanted to learn more about this soldier whose voice had been silenced so young, and about the daughter who never received her father's letter.

It took her fourteen years.

One day, a friend of a friend sent Donna a Facebook message. He had seen one of her posts. He knew of Eddington's great-great-grandson. It didn't take long before Donna could connect the family dots and was placing a phone call to sixty-nine-year-old Peggy Eddington-Smith in Dayton, Nevada.

Shocked and thankful, Peggy told Donna that she sadly knew almost nothing about her father. Her mother, heartbroken by her husband's death, had rarely, if ever, spoken of him, remaining unmarried until her death. She had told Peggy that she had met her "perfect man" and that no one else would ever compare.

Donna raised money herself to travel to Nevada to present the items—and the letter—to Peggy. She also reached out to the Nevada Patriot Guard in hopes of locating a living World War II veteran to formally present Peggy with the Purple Heart. Ninety-three-year-old Quentin McColl offered to help.

So, on Saturday, September 21, 2013, Donna Gregory, Quentin McColl, and a group of veterans and dignitaries arrived at the Dayton Intermediate School. In a ceremony held in the school's gym, Donna handed over the contents of the box to Peggy and her family.

A twenty-one-gun salute thundered outside and a trumpeter

played taps to honor John Farrell Eddington's final sacrifice. And out loud, Donna read the letter, which included the following:

My Darling Daughter,
You have never seen me or may never see me for some time. I'm sending you this so that you will always know that you have a very proud daddy somewhere in this world fighting for you and our country....I love you so much. We will always give you all the love we have....You have the sweetest mother on the Earth.

Donna concluded with the letter's last line: "I love you with all my heart and soul forever and forever. Your loving daddy."[1]

Have you ever gone back and looked at letters you've written?

Can you hear your own voice in the words? Do they remind you of how you felt in that moment when you put pen to paper? Can you imagine receiving a letter like the one Peggy received? Can you imagine someone from your past sending you a message?

And what if that letter was from *you*?

Your Scare Your Soul Commitment

Science tells us that the better we visualize our futures, the better the chance will be that we will achieve our goals. Anyone who has developed a five-year business plan or sat with cut-up magazines constructing a vision board knows how beneficial that work can be.

Call it planning, manifesting, goal setting, priming the law of attraction...when we articulate to ourselves the future that we want, we help create our future reality. It's all true.

But I am inviting you to do something even deeper and far more profound. Something that will, like Peggy's letter from her father, grow in value with age.

Scare Your Soul Challenge: Write a Letter to Yourself for the Journey Ahead

I invite you to write a letter to yourself that you can open or revisit exactly one year from now.

- Write boldly about how you will Scare Your Soul. How will this upcoming year be different?
- Write about what is scaring you now, and what you will do to overcome your fear. What leaps will you take?
- Get excited. What kind of adventures do you want to have? What kind of reconnections will you make? How do you want to grow? How will you serve others? How will courage lead to more authentic relationships?
- And if you wish, completely disregard it all and write the letter that you need to write.

In *The Alchemist*, Paulo Coelho wrote, "And, when you want something, all the universe conspires in helping you to achieve it."[2]

Write your letter. The universe has big ears. It will listen.

And here is a promise to you from me: I am here for you.

I honor your intentions and your vision. If you wish, email your letter to scott@scareyoursoul.com. Exactly one year from the day I receive it, I will email it back to you. When you receive your letter, it will become your time machine.

It will mark your journey.

That year when you first started to Scare Your Soul.

Jenn's Pilot Light Blazes

Everyone has a plan until they get punched in the mouth.

—MIKE TYSON

Fireworks went off as we all celebrated the new year of 2020. But as we all know, everyone has gotten punched in the mouth since then. Pandemic. Global recession. Social unrest. While trying to digest this all, I realized my energy was seeping because of loss. Not just loss of loved ones, but the loss of control, expectation, and hope.

My biggest loss happened when my business partner and best bud for twenty-plus years, Tony Hsieh, passed away. Tony and I had been in the space of happiness together for so long. Now, I knew there was a new place where "Delivering Happiness"—the company we co-founded—needed to go. A place that our community believed in…a place beyond happiness. What does happiness even mean today and how are we spending the precious minutes of our lives most meaningfully?

My Scare Your Soul moment happened at that time.

I was processing Tony's passing, all the loss in the world, and had to write a book that felt authentic to what I was observing and feeling. It seemed impossible to do all of those things justice. But, as I felt the steadfast support of people—strangers, my community, and loved ones—I was able to observe a lighter place within me.

That became my pilot light. It was a reminder that we all need to nurture our greenhouses as we grow others'. It's the oxygen mask we all need to put on, even when it feels counterintuitive. It was a testament to what living purpose and values—authentically within ourselves—can do for us, even in our darkest times.

What I now know more than ever is that it's the time we space for ourselves that makes the biggest difference. A walk outside. Riding a bike. Spending time with the people we love. Those everyday moments equate to the gratitude of all that we have, even when our soul gets scared.

Never forget—you'll always have your pilot light within, to shine with others.

Parting Thoughts

The best way out is always through. —ROBERT FROST

If you've ever taken an epic hike, at its conclusion is usually a vista—a breathtakingly delicious view, a payoff for all the miles you've traveled.

There's usually a still quietness. A rush of awareness. Like standing at the precipice of the Grand Canyon, taking it all in and feeling this beautiful sense of connectedness and completion... as if one long exhale into that void could somehow influence the winds.

Dear reader, that place is where you and I stand right now—the vista at the end of a journey, and the beginning of another.

Through this book, we have shared, reflected, challenged, and overcome. And there is so much more work to do, so many journeys of courage ahead. And so, I offer you thirty parting thoughts, collected in my spiral notebooks through my own courage adventure.

I hope they might be signposts for you along your way:

1. Growing and succeeding don't mean less fear; they mean more fear. They mean more new experiences you will have, people you will meet, ideas that will arise, and challenges you will face. Expect them. Enjoy them. They are why you are here.
2. Accountability is an underrated superpower. Find someone to hold you accountable, and do the same for them. It will become one of the strongest, most fruitful relationships in your life.
3. Boldly sharing your scariest truths will win you admirers and friends the world over.
4. Be limitless in your aspirations. When in doubt, dream big. Scale back as necessary. (Hint: It won't be necessary.)

5. Let me be clear: *you are needed.* Your family needs you. Your community needs you. The world needs you. Don't shrink back. Go forth boldly and bring us all your greatest gifts.

6. When you need to be brave in the moment, just ask yourself, *What would I do here if I literally could not fail?* That will tell you everything you need to know.

7. There's a hard conversation that needs to be had. You know the one. Have it.

8. People are not paying attention to you and judging. They're caught up in their own movie.

9. When you're scared, ask yourself, *What am I afraid of losing here?* When we allow ourselves to be free of our attachments (our possessions, ego, status), those fears begin to drift away like water.

10. Remember that some desired future outcome is your enemy. Action, not outcome, is where the gold lies.

11. Get lost on purpose. That's where you will find some of the best things in life.

12. When you're overwhelmed, find excellence in the tiniest action you can imagine. Even making a bed can be done with both panache and precision.

13. Enduring just ten seconds of outrageous anxiety (or embarrassment or awkwardness) is often the gateway to something really amazing.

14. Find small ways to connect with others every single day (especially when it feels hard). Smile at strangers, compliment people, remind others that they are making a difference. You're creating ripples of goodness.

15. When it comes to your own growth, be completely and unapologetically selfish.

16. Write your own eulogy at least once a year. Remembering your mortality isn't morbid. It's a key to bold vitality.

17. When you start and fail, remember the wise counsel of meditation teachers over the millennia: "It's all OK. Just begin again."

18. When you feel scared and unable to act, focus yourself in a role of service. Your act, in some way, is making someone's life—or the world—better.

19. When you think you are stuck, you're not. You have choices. Just sit awhile. They will present themselves soon enough.

20. Human beings are incredibly resilient. So, fail big. Don't die with opportunities still waiting inside you.

21. Following through on promises to others is really important. Following through on promises to yourself is essential.

22. Just as change is exciting, it is hard. In moments of transition, remember what Joseph Campbell said: "We must let go of the life we've planned so as to have the life that is waiting for us."[3]

23. Be stringent about who gets time in your life. Add people who inspire and motivate; subtract complainers and critics. You decide who gets the blessing of your time.

24. From time to time, become a complete beginner at something. Embrace the simplicity of not knowing.

25. Breathe. Breathe. Breathe.

26. Possessions don't make us happy. Growth does.

27. "When one door closes, another opens" isn't just an aphorism. It's unadulterated truth.

28. Don't pretend to know what is going to happen in life; none of us knows. It's OK. Just move forward.

29. Learn the difference between instant gratification and pleasure. Avoid the sugary jolt of the quick moment; live, instead, for what brings you deep, sustained pleasure.

30. You don't need to "achieve" to be able to celebrate. Once in a while, just sit, breathe, and smile. You're doing your best. Celebrate THAT.

Dear reader, it has been an honor to be alongside you in the greatest work that any of us can do.

As we part, I will share with you the immortal words of John Wayne: "Courage is being scared to death, and saddling up anyway."

I encourage you in your bold journey ahead.

I wish you years full of gratitude, adventure, energy, curiosity, awe, forgiveness, and meaningful work.

And I hope you don't ever stop Scaring Your Soul.

Deeper Practice

If you have interest in continuing your experience with Scare Your Soul, here are a few suggestions for an ongoing experience.

1. Create an online journal of your thoughts, reflections, and challenges at www.scareyoursoul.com.
2. Receive free weekly challenges by joining the Scare Your Soul courage movement at www.scareyoursoul.com and follow our exploits on Instagram at www.instagram.com/scareyoursoul.
3. Read this book in tandem with an accountability partner. Share the reflections and prompts and do the Scare Your Soul challenges together.
4. Create a Scare Your Soul book group. Read the book sequentially or pick chapters that interest the group. Use the content as the jumping off point for rich conversation.
5. Gift this book to someone in your life who needs it.
6. Write a review about this book on your favorite online bookseller's website.
7. When you do something brave, proudly let someone know that you "scared your soul."
8. Create your own Scare Your Soul group in your community. Reach out to us at contact@scareyoursoul.com and we will help you bring it to reality.

Notes

Introduction

1. Mary Oliver, *New and Selected Poems* (Boston: Beacon Press, 2004).

Chapter 1

1. Viktor Emil Frankl, *Man's Search for Meaning: An Introduction to Logotherapy*, a newly rev. and enl. ed. of *From Death-Camp to Existentialism*, trans. Ilse Lasch, pref. by Gordon W. Allport (Boston: Beacon Press, 1970).
2. "Elizabeth Gilbert: The Creative Life," Good Life Project, accessed January 31, 2022, https://www.goodlifeproject.com/podcast/elizabeth-gilbert/.

Chapter 4

1. R. E. Boyatzis, M. Smith, and E. Van Oosten, *Helping People Change: Coaching with Compassion for Lifelong Learning and Growth* (Cambridge: Harvard Business Review Press, 2019).
2. L. A. King, "The Health Benefits of Writing about Life Goals," *Personality and Social Psychology Bulletin* 27, no. 7 (2001): 798–807, https://doi.org/10.1177/0146167201277003.

Chapter 5

1. D. J. Siegel, *Brainstorm: The Power and Purpose of the Teenage Brain* (New York: Jeremy P. Tarcher/Penguin, 2013).
2. Naomi I. Eisenberger et al., "Neural Pathways Link Social Support to Attenuated Neuroendocrine Stress Responses," *NeuroImage* 35 (2007), https://www.scn.ucla.edu/pdf/Eisenberger%20et%20al%202007.pdf.
3. L. M. Rankin, *The Fear Cure: Cultivating Courage as Medicine for the Body, Mind, and Soul* (Carlsbad, CA: Hay House Inc., 2015).
4. C. S. Dweck, *Mindset: Changing the Way You Think to Fulfil Your Potential* (New York: Little, Brown Book Group, 2017).

Chapter 6

1. D. Chen, "This Is the Real Reason You Procrastinate—and How to Break the Habit," ideas.ted.com., March 12, 2020, https://ideas.ted.com/this-is-the-real-reason-you-procrastinate-and-how-to-break-the-habit/.

2. J. Stillman, "'Handmaid's Tale' Author and Self-Described Lazy Person Margaret Atwood Explains How She Beats Procrastination," *Inc.com.*, March 24, 2020, https://www.inc.com/jessica-stillman/handmaids-tale-author -self-described-lazy-person-margaret-atwood-explains-how-she-beats -procrastination.html.

3. A. W. Brooks, "Get Excited: Reappraising Pre-performance Anxiety as Excitement," *Journal of Experimental Psychology* 143, no. 3 (2014), https:// www.apa.org/pubs/journals/releases/xge-a0035325.pdf.

4. "The Work Is a Practice," The Work of Byron Katie, accessed January 23, 2022, https://thework.com/instruction-the-work-byron-katie/.

5. "Four Liberating Questions," The Work of Byron Katie, October 16, 2017, https://thework.com/2017/10/four-liberating-questions/.

Chapter 7

1. J. C. Maxwell, *Failing Forward: How to Make the Most of Your Mistakes* (Nashville: Thomas Nelson Publishers, 2000).

2. Sandi Mann, *Why Do I Feel like an Imposter?: How to Understand and Cope with Imposter Syndrome* (London: Watkins Publishing, 2019).

3. Valerie Young, *The Secret Thoughts of Successful Women: Why Capable People Suffer from the Impostor Syndrome and How to Thrive in Spite of It* (New York: Crown Business, 2011).

4. "Impostor Phenomenon," on Pauline Rose Clance's official website, accessed February 6, 2022, https://paulineroseclance.com/impostor_phenomenon .html.

5. "Good C.E.O.'s Are Insecure (and Know It)," *New York Times,* Oct. 10, 2010, Section BU, Page 2, https://www.nytimes.com/2010/10/10/business /10corner.html?_r=1.

6. Dr. Margie Warrell, "Afraid of Being 'Found Out'? How to Overcome Impostor Syndrome," *Forbes* magazine, April 3, 2014, https://www.forbes.com /sites/margiewarrell/2014/04/03/impostor-syndrome/?sh=3d0e227548a9.

7. Annie Yuan, "HBO Releases New Preview for Lady Gaga Documentary," *The Hollywood Reporter,* April 24, 2011, https://www.hollywoodreporter .com/news/music-news/hbo-releases-new-preview-lady-181733/.

8. Neil A. Lewis, "On a Supreme Court Prospect's Résumé: 'Baseball Savior,'" *New York Times*, May 14, 2009, https://www.nytimes.com/2009/05/15 /us/15sotomayor.html.

9. "Tom Hanks Says Self-Doubt Is 'A High-Wire Act That We All Walk,'" *Fresh Air* (Produced by WHYY in Philadelphia), NPR, April 26, 2016. https:// www.npr.org/2016/04/26/475573489/tom-hanks-says-self-doubt-is-a-high -wire-act-that-we-all-walk.

10. D. LaPorte, *The Fire Starter Sessions: A Soulful + Practical Guide to Creating Success on Your Own Terms* (New York: Harmony Books, 2014).

Chapter 8

1. Robert Emmons, "Why Gratitude Is Good," *Greater Good Magazine*, November 16, 2010, https://greatergood.berkeley.edu/article/item/why_gratitude_is_good.
2. Edward N. Lorenz, "Deterministic Nonperiodic Flow," *Journal of Atmospheric Sciences* 20, no. 2 (March 1, 1963), https://journals.ametsoc.org/view/journals/atsc/20/2/1520-0469_1963_020_0130_dnf_2_0_co_2.xml.

Chapter 9

1. "Tommy Rivs: The Poet of Endurance Rages On: Surviving Cancer, the Gift of Pain & the Healing Power of Gratitude," Rich Roll podcast, episode 648, October 13, 2021, https://www.richroll.com/podcast/tommy-rivs-648/.
2. Talya Minsberg, "Cancer Nearly Took His Life. But the New York Marathon Awaited," *New York Times*, November 8, 2021, https://www.nytimes.com/2021/11/08/sports/tommy-rivers-puzey-marathon.html.
3. Martin Buber, *The Legend of the Baal-Shem* (London: Routledge, 2002).
4. "Tommy Rivs: The Poet of Endurance Rages On."
5. R. Agrawal, *Belong: Find Your People, Create Community, and Live a More Connected Life* (New York: Workman Publishing Co., Inc., 2019).
6. Gina Shaw, "Marilu Henner's Exceptional Memory Spurs Interest in Brain Health," *Brain and Life Magazine*, February/March 2019, https://www.brainandlife.org/articles/actress-marilu-henner-has-a-highly-superior-autobiographical-memory-a/.
7. Julie Marquis, "UCI Study Ties Memory to Emotion," *Los Angeles Times*, October 20, 1994, https://www.latimes.com/archives/la-xpm-1994-10-20-mn-52568-story.html.

Chapter 10

1. Jack Kornfield, "Spiritual Life Takes Courage," on Jack Kornfield's official website, accessed January 25, 2022, https://jackkornfield.com/spiritual-life-takes-courage/.
2. A. S.-K. Pang, *Rest: Why You Get More Done When You Work Less* (New York: Basic Books, 2018).

Chapter 11

1. R. Waldinger, *"What Makes a Good Life? Lessons from the Longest Study on Happiness,"* TEDxBeaconStreet, TED, November 2015, https://www

.ted.com/talks/robert_waldinger_what_makes_a_good_life_lessons
_from_the_longest_study_on_happiness.

2. J. McGregor, "This Former Surgeon General Says There's a 'Loneliness Epi-demic' and Work Is Partly to Blame," *Washington Post*, October 4, 2017, https://www.washingtonpost.com/news/on-leadership/wp/2017/10/04 /this-former-surgeon-general-says-theres-a-loneliness-epidemic-and -work-is-partly-to-blame/.

3. Anis Mojgani, "These Things Are How You Make Me Feel," Genius, accessed January 26, 2022, https://genius.com/Anis-mojgani-these-things -are-how-you-make-me-feel-annotated.

4. Meeri Kim, "Cats, Take Notice: Brain Study Uses Trivia to Look at How Curiosity Works," *Washington Post*, October 5, 2014, https://www .washingtonpost.com/national/health-science/cats-take-notice-brain -study-uses-trivia-to-look-at-how-curiosity-works/2014/10/05/7c9eccfe -4b38-11e4-a046-120a8a855cca_story.html.

5. R. Britten, *Fearless Living: Live without Excuses and Succeed beyond Your Dreams* (Hodder Headline, 2001).

6. M. L. Catron, "To Fall in Love with Anyone, Do This," *New York Times*, January 9, 2015, https://www.nytimes.com/2015/01/11/style/modern-love -to-fall-in-love-with-anyone-do-this.html.

Chapter 12

1. Ralph Waldo Emerson and Larzer Ziff, *Nature and Selected Essays* (Pen-guin Books Ltd, 2003).

2. Abraham H. Maslow, *Religions, Values, and Peak-Experiences* (New York: Viking Press, 1973).

3. G. Plimpton, "Fireworks by Plimpton!," *Vanity Fair*, July 1984, https://archive .vanityfair.com/article/share/0a829395-2341-4a91-a580-3d99892659d8.

4. Abraham Joshua Heschel, *God in Search of Man: A Philosophy of Judaism* (New York: Farrar, Straus and Giroux, 2000).

Chapter 13

1. F. Luskin, "The Art of Forgiveness," Surviving Cancer, Stanford Center for Integrative Medicine, accessed January 25, 2022, https://med.stanford .edu/survivingcancer/coping-with-cancer/cancer-and-forgiveness .html.

2. K. Corrigan, "If You Think You Can't Forgive, Remember, You Do It All the Time," *New York Times*, November 24, 2021, https://www.nytimes.com /2021/11/24/opinion/thanksgiving-family-forgiveness.html.

3. Mayo Clinic Staff, "Forgiveness: Letting Go of Grudges and Bitterness," Mayo Clinic, November 13, 2020, https://www.mayoclinic.org/healthy-lifestyle/adult-health/in-depth/forgiveness/art-20047692.

4. K. Nerburn, *Calm Surrender: Walking the Path of Forgiveness* (New World Library, 2002).

5. S. Salzberg, *Lovingkindness: The Revolutionary Art of Happiness* (Boulder: Shambhala, 2020).

Chapter 16

1. Associated Press, "WWII Soldier's Letter Finally Reaches Daughter," *Lubbock Avalanche-Journal*, September 21, 2013, https://www.lubbockonline.com/story/news/nation-world/2013/09/22/wwii-soldiers-letter-finally-reaches-daughter/15073890007/.

2. Paulo Coelho, *The Alchemist: A Fable about Following Your Dream* (New York: HarperCollins Publishers, 2016).

3. Joseph Campbell and Diane K. Osbon, *A Joseph Campbell Companion: Reflections on the Art of Living* (New York: HarperCollins, 1991).

Index

About the Author

Photo © Kim Ponsky

Scott Simon is a happiness entrepreneur, speaker, and founder of Scare Your Soul, a movement inspiring individual and global change through small acts of courage. He has spoken around the world, motivated people at schools and companies, given a TEDx talk, co-founded a happiness incubator, and studied and worked with international thought leaders in the areas of courage and happiness. He is a high-performance coach, focusing primarily on creating flourishing lives post divorce; leads mindfulness meditations; and has served as an officiant of numerous weddings. Scott earned his BA from Skidmore College, his MA from Case Western Reserve University, and certificates in positive psychology and coaching from the Wholebeing Institute. Scott is the proud father of two children, and when not out fulfilling his sense of wanderlust, he lives in Cleveland, Ohio.